The Golf Course:
Planning, Design, Construction and Maintenance

The Golf Course:
Planning, Design, Construction and Maintenance

F. W. Hawtree

London   New York

E. & F. N. SPON

First published 1983 by
E. & F.N. Spon Ltd
11 New Fetter Lane
London EC4P 4EE

Published in the USA by
E. & F.N. Spon
733 Third Avenue
New York NY 10017

Printed in Great Britain
at the University Press, Cambridge

ISBN 0 419 12250 8

British Library Cataloguing in Publication Data

Hawtree, F.W.
    The golf course.
    1. Golf courses – design and construction
    I. Title
    796.352'06'8   GV975

    ISBN 0-419-12250-8

Library of Congress Cataloging in Publication Data

Hawtree, F. W. (Fred W.)
    The golf course.

    Bibliography: p.
    Includes index.
    1. Golf courses—Design and construction.
    2. Landscape architecture.   I. Title.
GV975.H38 1983   796.352'06'8   82-19143
ISBN 0-419-12250-8

Contents

Foreword   vii
Acknowledgements   ix

1 Introduction   1

2 Philosophy   4
2.1 The formative years   4
2.2 The Middle Age   30
2.3 Transition   35
2.4 Lessons   40

3 Planning   46
3.1 The site   46
3.2 Layout   49
3.3 Guidelines   55
3.4 Rehearsal   58
3.5 Short alternatives   61

4 Design   64
4.1 Tees   64
4.2 Putting greens   85
4.3 Bunkers   111
4.4 Fairways and rough   122
4.5 Trees   126
4.6 Water   139

5 Construction   145
5.1 Method   145
5.2 Specification   149
5.3 Bills of Quantity   151
5.4 Drawings   153
5.5 Clerk of Works   154

6 Practical politics   156
6.1 The head greenkeeper   156
6.2 Etiquette   159
6.3 Safety   162
6.4 Furniture   163
6.5 Presentation   165
6.6 A single green   171

Appendix 1   177
Survey of the carry (pitch) of drives
carried out on behalf of the
British Association of Golf Course
Architects (B.A.G.C.A.)

Appendix 2   178
Length/area guide

Appendix 3   179
Green plans (Martin G. Hawtree)

Appendix 4   183
Specimen pages: Specification and Bills
of Quantity

Appendix 5
Tree lists   195

Appendix 6
Metric/Imperial conversions   203

Bibliography   205

Index   208

Foreword

Henry Cotton MBE

At the start, I must tell the reader that this book is a detailed, interesting study of how to design and build a golf course – a complex business.

The author's father entered golf course design through greenkeeping and in the 1920s joined up with that great golfer, J.H. Taylor. Theirs were some of the first modern inland courses, away from the links where Nature had already prepared the way. I particularly remember some of that original planning, with island greens completely surrounded by a ring of sand-traps, obliging golfers to approach by the all-air route and calling for nominated shots.

The present Fred Hawtree (son of Hawtree I) and his son, Martin, have carried on the practice of golf course architecture, living with golf and doing their work with skill and good taste. This book will help golfers and officials to improve their personal ideas on layout, especially those with low handicaps and their own interests at heart.

There are many amateur golf course architects who seek to alter holes they dislike; some I have known have even become golf club officials in order to fill in a hazard which regularly collects one of their shots. In the face of such pressures, Hawtree courses (and they have owned one as well as designed hundreds) are fair but never easy to handle.

Fred Hawtree 'knows his stuff' and this book is a classic.

Portimao
January 1983

Acknowledgements

The sources of conscious quotations are, I hope, all acknowledged in the text but some deserve special mention.

The Game of Golf, by Willie Park Junr., (Longmans, Green & Co, London, 1896) broke new ground as, indeed, did his seventy odd golf courses in America and one of the earliest combined housing and golf course developments at Huntercombe.

Garden G. Smith's *The World of Golf* (A.D. Innes & Co., London 1898) was also a source of much stimulating material.

John Laing Low codified the best principles of golf course architecture in *Concerning Golf* (Hodder & Stoughton, London, 1903) and his work at Woking helped to establish the profession.

Country Life, as the original source, kindly gave permission to quote from *Golf Greens and Greenkeeping* (Country Life & George Newnes Ltd. London, 1906).

The 'Great Triumvirate' contributed strong professional views over the first half of this century. J.H.'s *Taylor on Golf* (Hutchinson & Co. London, 1902) James Braid's *Advanced Golf* (1908) and Harry Vardon's *How to Play Golf*, 1912, (both published by Methuen & Co. London) have all been of assistance.

Messrs. Suttons Seeds Ltd. were good enough to permit quoting from *The Book of the Links* edited by Martin H.F. Sutton (W.H. Smith & Son, London, 1912).

My thanks are due also to Dr Alister Mackenzie's *Golf Architecture* (Simpkin, Marshall, Hamilton & Co, London, 1920) and *The Architectural Side of Golf*, by H.N. Wethered & T. Simpson (Longmans Green & Co, London, 1929).

There is much more to write about these books and others I have listed as, indeed, there is about colleagues whose joint efforts founded the British Association of Golf Course Architects with the encouragement of George McPartlin and the Golf Development Council.

My father founded the British Golf Greenkeepers Association in 1912. The first generation have long departed: men like A.G. Whitall, Woodcote Park; Arthur Lacey, Burnham Beeches and later, Ifield; Charles Prickett, Frilford Heath. I have, however, been fortunate to profit from the collaboration of many others: Cyril Chamberlain and Bill Machin while I had the Addington Court Golf Club; George Herrington, Lindrick; Franz Knekkerbroek, Royal Waterloo; Douglas Pate, Royal Birkdale; Harry Smith, Bruntsfield; George Wilson, Le Prieuré, Paris. Some, alas, died in harness as did Jim Ellis, St Nom la Bretèche and Ted Macavoy, Hillside, due partly, I believe, to their excess of zeal in setting the scene for their members before standing modestly aside.

Raymond Read kindly gave permission for the use of his measurements in Appendix I. Messrs. Ransomes, Sims, Jefferies, Ipswich, generously provided photographs from their library, and I am also grateful to H.W. Neale (Action Photos, Sutton, Surrey) for twelve more. It has been impossible to trace the authors of all the illustrations but I hope that the acknowledgements given to golf clubs will at least identify them locally. Those of Mortonhall in Edinburgh illustrate not only the skills of the photographer but also of Douglas Horn who supervised the work.

Last and first, Henry Cotton MBE, a champion golfer in the classic mould, and golf course architect himself, generously consented to contribute a foreword and kept his promise in the midst of a sudden, grievous sorrow.

To all of these and to many others who have uncovered the fascinations of the golf course, my grateful thanks for their influence on this book. It needed only five more valued collaborators:

> Phillip Read suggested it;
> F.G. Hawtree really began it;
> Alan Bibby indexed it;
> Martin Hawtree improved it;
> And, hardest of all, Mary Hawtree lived with it.

1 Introduction

This book is first of all about golf course architecture. It begins with the writings of the earliest architects of golf courses because their books are not easily come by and the similarity of their philosophy and ours is of significance. Having mostly the same aims, their results were noticeably different but this is probably of less significance, given the infinite variety of their sites and local variations in interpreting their instructions.

Their successors have written far less on the subject and, indeed, there comes an early limit to what can usefully be said about golf course architecture in general. This has led to the second aim of these pages. I have tried to expand the subject into specific sections which may be of wider use to those thousands of golfers who every year, after peacefully and anonymously enjoying their golf in the rank and file of members, allow themselves to be elected to the Green Committee. There are not many guide books to help them find their way through these byways of golf although there are almost too many advising them how to play it.

In Scotland, their leader will be called Green Convener – a neater, more musical term than Chairman of the Green Committee. It also emphasizes that the 'Green' referred to is the whole course not one of eighteen small parts of it. That distinction, regrettably, is lost in solecisms like 'Greens Chairman'. 'Greens Committee' and, worst of all, 'Greens-Keeper'. This error by analogy is mostly found in lands where the greenkeeper has graduated to 'Course Superintendent', 'Course Manager' and 'Curator'.

We have perhaps been backward in British greenkeeping in providing the intensive training, the degree courses and research which have produced so many talented golf course superintendents in the United States and elsewhere; but there has been an immense fund of solid experience handed down from which the profession in the British Isles has moved steadily forward. 'Greenkeeper' is still an honourable title. It might only be regretted that the term 'Clubmaster', which became 'Steward' when it crossed the border, was not matched by 'Greenmaster' for the man who cared for the course.

The term 'Green Convener' will be used here out of deference to the Scots who invented the game of golf. We cannot thank them enough. But the Green Chairman (or, simply, Chairman) and the Green Committee will equally be present. 'Le Président de la Commission du Parcours', 'der Präsident des Greenvorstandes', 'el Capitán del Campo', and their Committees are also invited to these meetings. They are all welcome.

The election of the Green Convener will reflect personal qualities, whether they be leadership,. bonhomie or business acumen; or he may, unwisely, have talked himself into the job by the frequent expression of strong views. Often it is a stepping stone to subsequent captaincy. Sometimes it derives from his principal occupation: a farmer will be expected to know about turf – an engineer, about machinery. I am not one who believes that the chairman of a specialist committee should necessarily be an expert on the subjects under review. An incisive, analytical mind will soon draw out, compare and balance the opinions of the experts assembled. But where the members of a committee are themselves equally new and unversed in the matters requiring decision, it seems to be desirable that its chairman should have some background knowledge to enable him to guide the discussion; and this will be still more fruitful if his committee has done some homework as well.

This book is intended to help them with those tasks, but it ranges wider than the immediate problems they will have to decide. The early philosophy of the game will be reviewed because it is still relevant and should colour an approach to today's debates. Similarly, the section on the architecture of the golf course will start from the virgin site and first principles in order to help in understanding why the course now under their wing is in its present form.

There will be no discussion of golf greenkeeping except in so far as it is affected by architectural and constructional decisions. There are useful books and periodicals on maintenance (see *Bibliography*) and a great deal of research is in progress. Nevertheless, head greenkeepers may find this book of interest in broadening the horizons against which they measure their daily tasks and help them to prepare the ground for the fruits of that research.

Similarly, the golf club professional, being generally the best player in the club, will often be the testing ground for new ideas about the golf course. The Professional Golfers Association runs instructional courses which very sensibly instruct young professionals in far more aspects of golf club activities than the bare essentials of golf shop, repairs and tuition. The successful professional's role is becoming much broader and the more rounded his knowledge, the more constructively he can operate in the role of confessor and confidant, as his father and grandfather used to do.

Lastly, the man in the front line, the secretary or manager can never have enough bricks to build his defences against those with a modest taste for improvements or to throw at those with ideas more extravagant. For this reason, he will find quoted a variety of aphorisms from the past as well as the asseverations of the present, in case the latter fail to be convincing.

I have tried, however, to avoid excursions into the history of the game as such, its development abroad, and the influence of Scots like Donald Ross, who translated the essence of Dornoch golf into so many North American layouts. The history has been written many times before and there is little to add that is new. The threads of golf course architecture which run through it have been unravelled and lavishly rewoven by my friend, Geoffrey Cornish, and Ronald E. Whitten in their encyclopaedic survey *The Golf Course* published in 1981, where the keen student will also find the world's golf courses and their designers, often united in print for the first time.

These pages are, therefore, principally dedicated to all the little teams of four or five who work to ensure the golfing satisfaction of a hundred times their number. As in other fields, one is frequently puzzled by their abdication from the peace and freedom of ordinary membership. But, again, as in other fields, they will give the unassailable answer: 'Somebody had to do it!' Long may it be so.

The principal headings in the text broadly describe the material grouped under them. But there are many interrelated factors where planning affects design, or design affects construction, or construction affects both of the others, and such combinations are taken as seems appropriate.

If occasionally (and one hopes it is only occasionally), the advice seems unduly portentous for the subject matter, let it always be remembered that, in the words of P. G. Wodehouse's heroine, 'It's only a game, isn't it?'

2 Philosophy

'King James IV took up golf about
1490. This was really in the 15th
Century, but for some reason time
travels faster than dates.'

A pupil of Mike Collins, physical education
teacher, quoted in the *USGA Golf Journal*

2.1 THE FORMATIVE YEARS

Most of the philosophy of planning and design which we accept today as gospel was set out between 1896 and 1920 by four professional and four amateur golfers, none of whom had been trained in any of the disciplines associated with golf course architecture beyond personal experience of play. Presumably, through that ability, they recognized what gave pleasure, interest, excitement, boredom, irritation, or fatigue and steered a way through the problems of building the course with an eye firmly fixed on the eventual golfer. He is still the final judge. But they were soon preaching the virtues of variety, avoidance of formality and the imitation of Nature, which had inspired landscape designers of more than a century before. What they wrote has been rewritten again and again in differing forms but we have not added much new.

Construction techniques, however, especially earth-moving, have advanced to the point where, if necessary, sites formerly considered unsuitable, like rubbish tips, can be landscaped, planted, and transformed into things of beauty – at a cost. But more ordinary, economical projects will be those where careful planning and selection of routes and green positions will display to best advantage the assets which the site already possesses. This approach was essential to all the earliest architects.

Fig. 2.1   The first Ransomes 'Triple' mower had a cut of seven feet and in 1924 cost £125 (£210 for a quintuple), carriage paid to any railway station. This one is standing in front of the Gleneagles Hotel. The horses normally wore leather boots to reduce surface damage. (Courtesy of Ransomes Sims Jefferies plc.)

Before horses and scoops were called in, all insisted that their first duty was to employ fully all the natural features of the site.

There are still important issues which endanger that attitude, not the least alarming being that the extravagant transformation of sites, which is possible where related development will foot the bill can become the expected norm elsewhere. Plans for new projects will then price themselves out of the market. We have to reverse fashion by getting back to the simplicity and subtlety of the site itself.

Many of the matters on which the first golfing architects pronounced are still being argued today. There has indeed been a steady progress away from blind holes as they all correctly forecast, but two views about rough were current then and, theoretically, still are today. How short the short hole? How long the par 5? Is a tree a fair hazard? Is a visible bunker fair even in the middle of the fairway at the end of a good drive? All these questions survive – thank goodness!

One remorseless advance has been the apparent improvement of turf, or perhaps we should say 'playing conditions'. We have reached a stage now where modern cultivated turf is thought inferior to the old natural cover being botanically less desirable and less hard-wearing. On the other hand, the degree of use in earlier times never really confirmed the durability of the natural cover or its ability to recover quickly. Many links courses today are sadly worn even in the carry rough.

The Green Committee must face up to this dilemma at local level in order to preserve the course and the peace. It is not a new one as a backward glance will show.

The practice of golf course architecture might be thought to have begun in 1764 when the St Andrews golfers decided to reduce their course from 11 holes to 9, that is to say from 22 to 18, out and home. The change may have been made for practical reasons or to produce two longer holes of 390 yards more in line with the average length which was 350. They must have been woefully short as opening and climax to the circuit. The decision may, at the same time, have been influenced by memories of the games of Nine Holes, Nine Pins, and even Nine Men's Morris. The number has a certain mysterious significance in many games, indoors and out.

The influence of the precedent course at Leith, however, continued well into the 19th Century and, when it was extended from five to seven holes in 1844, Blackheath did the same (Fig. 2.2). This

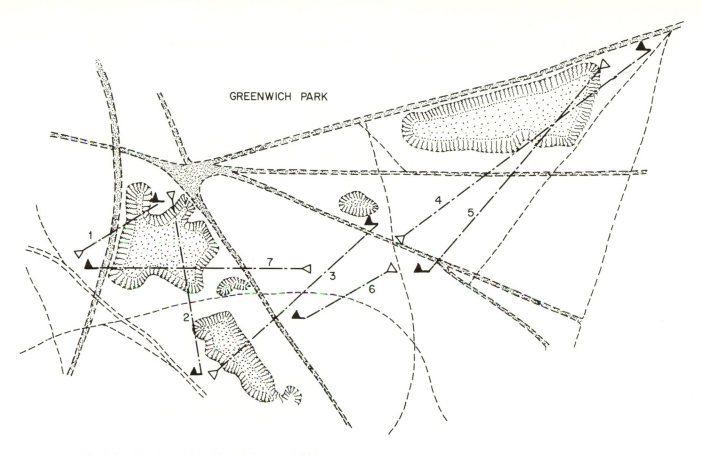

GREENWICH PARK

Fig. 2.2 The Royal Blackheath layout, 1844.

must have been a total replanning and the true start of marrying and modelling land to the essential interest of the game which is golf course architecture. The original five hole course avoided all the quarries on the heath because they were still being worked. On the new course every hole played over a quarry except no. 6. The engraving *Medal Day at Blackheath* shows quarry, traffic and passers-by beyond the well-dressed players standing on the tee.

The card read:
170
335
380
540
500
230
410
———
2565 Yards

Oddly enough, this series of lengths breaks several of the rules which later planners consider should form the ideal pattern. More oddly still, it is often where the rules are broken that a golf course becomes notable. Perhaps those pioneers knew what amused the public better than their successors. The miracle of golf was the synthesis in opposition, as in no other game, of the long and the short, the strong and the weak, the brash and the canny, skill and chance, rough and smooth. At the start it was certainly rough. Now we may be in danger of it becoming too smooth.

The second half of the 19th Century saw a mighty expansion in golf courses, but not in designers. To try to assess prevailing attitudes we can only turn to *The Golfing Annual* which started in 1887 with 226 pages and grew to 760 pages by 1909, even with entries much condensed. It would be convenient for the historian if the overriding emphasis on hazards in most early entries evaporated as the years went by. But mood and attitudes change slowly and at different rates in different circumstances.

One detects, nevertheless, a growing improvement in the condition of courses, due to a nascent desire for so-called 'equity', a battle still being fought in the Rules as well as by Green Committees. There were die-hards who scorned this weakness and revelled in descriptions of dreadful hazards. But I suspect that the worse the condition of the course, the more the virtues of its hazards were extolled. Indeed, from the beginning, some of the older Scottish courses are already talking about playing conditions rather than playing adventures, even when match-play was the rule. (The italics are mine; the dates are those of foundation.)

Luffness (1876):
'The course is about two and three-quarter miles in length and is extremely difficult, being thickly interspersed with bunkers, ditches, and other hazards. The soil is of a very light sandy nature, with the exception of some of the low lying holes. The rabbits are very numerous, and their little scrapes render many a ball unplayable. The putting greens on the whole are *very fair, several of them having turf fit for a bowling green, and almost dead level.* Those at the sixth and seventh holes are, perhaps, as difficult as can be found anywhere, owing to their position on the slope of the hill, and to their being pretty well surrounded with bunkers. . . . Ditches and bunkers are placed at many of the holes in very awkward positions for medium drivers, but by a little judicious play these hazards can generally be avoided.'

But at Carnoustie (1842) the hazards were by 1887 causing little comment compared with the state of the putting greens.

'Carnoustie Golf links are, for a thorough display of the game in all its departments, second only to those at St Andrew's: indeed, some of our foremost golfers have declared that they prefer the former. There are eighteen holes in the round, the longest of which is 390 yards, and the shortest 210 yards, the total length being 5030 yds, or close upon three miles. The turf as a rule is excellently suited for the game, and there are hazards enough in the shape of bunkers – both natural and made up – to satisfy even the best, if not the worst of players. Much labour has been expended in getting the course and especially the putting greens into *the best possible order*. Many of these greens are in *grand condition*, and, in the case of the others, their present imperfect state is due to a recent extension of the course. They are however, *being speedily improved.'*

If we move on to Volume VII (1893/4), the newer inland clubs are still emphasizing hazards while apologizing for conditions. At Perth (1821), there had been more time for improvement but even so there comes a caveat.

'The game at Perth is played over the North Inch, a lovely expanse of turf on the border of the River Tay. Like all inland greens, play is confined to the Spring and Autumn months. The round consists of twelve holes. The turf is certainly not so good as at some of the seaside links'.

Eltham, south of London had, however, fared better.

'The course, originally laid out with eleven, was extended to eighteen holes, without any crossing, in the spring of 1893, and is about $3\frac{1}{4}$ miles long. The holes vary in length from about 125 to 450 yds, are well protected by sand bunkers, ponds, and other hazards; and the high opinions formed by experts at the outset have been well borne out by the excellent condition into which the green has now been brought.'

The Royal Blackheath Golf Club settled at Eltham when, like their Scottish predecessors, they had to leave public land as public interference with their game became excessive. But there was no quarter at Limpsfield Chart in Surrey (1889) where the land was both public and had not improved so much.

'The turf is not so perfectly suited to the requirements of the game, as in summer it is liable to be overgrown by grass and fern. This difficulty, however, has been met by the energy of the Green Committee, and the course is now in *fairly good order*. The distance of the round is nearly two miles, none of the holes being more than 350 yds in length, and none less than 150. The chief hazards are gorse bushes, but, with the exception of a few holes, the direct line from the tee to the disc is clear from such dangers. Before one or two of the teeing-grounds, however, there yawn even more formidable difficulties . . . Roads also, have to be crossed on several occasions and the ruts left by the carts which cross the common in all directions form a serious danger.'

The danger now affects road-users rather than golfers, one green being still only some six feet from traffic. (When I showed it to Bob Graves, the American golf course architect based in California, he took photographs in order to be able to convince any at home who doubted his veracity. Bob's daughter, Victoria, is probably the only woman in the world with a father and a husband in this profession, though in different firms.)

At Pau (1856), the oldest golf course on the continent of Europe, the hazards still get a mention, but not the turf. Location is beginning to count.

'The course, of eighteen holes, with *capital hazards*, . . . is within one mile of the town.'

One last quotation shows that the British Navy at least, had the right philosophy.

Gibraltar (1891):
'The course, of nine holes, is situated three miles from Gibraltar, adjoining the Spanish village of Campamento. By kind permission of the Naval Commander-in-Chief, members of the Golf Club are permitted to use the duty steam boat which runs to Campamento every day when the fleet is in.'

These examples and the sites of early links show that the genius of golf course architecture was very much the *genius loci* just as in the 18th Century, according to M.F. Downing (*Landscape Construction*, 1978), 'it was the guiding principle of all designers, and those improving their country house parks. Nature "imitated in any measure . . . gives us a nobler and more exalted kind of pleasure than what we receive from the nicer and more accurate Productions of Art". (Addison, 1712).'

Sir John Vanbrugh must have made one of the earliest acknowledgements of the value of natural site attributes in his reference to the grounds at Castle Howard which he had laid out, and of which he said 'I may commend them because Nature made them: I pretend to no more merit in them than a Midwife, who helps bring a fine child into the world out of the bushes, Boggs, and Bryars'.

Golf, on the contrary, first got on to the ground by accident rather than by design and has been trying to get itself right ever since. Before the 20th Century, no amateur golfers took up golf course architecture and only one elaborated its first principles, Old Tom Morris laid out Dornoch, the New

Course at St Andrews, the early form of Muirfield, and Machrihanish; Tom Dunn laid out Wimbledon; George Morris, the original nine at Hoylake. But Willie Park was the first professional to codify the attributes of good golf course design in a book, *The Game of Golf* (1896): only one chapter, but it contained sound and modest advice:

> 'The laying out of a golf course is by no means a simple task. Great skill and judgement, and a thorough acquaintance with the game are absolutely necessary to determine the best positions for the respective holes and teeing-grounds and the situation of the hazard.
>
> When a new course is to be laid out I would strongly advise the promoters to obtain the assistance of some one experienced in such matters.' (This can still be good advice a hundred years later.)
>
> 'If there be sufficient space for eighteen good holes so much the better; but if not, I would recommend that the number be fixed at either nine or six, as twice round the one and three times round the other completes the game. Fifteen and twelve-hole courses are sometimes found, but in either case the number is awkward. . . .
>
> It is desirable that the first teeing-ground and the last putting green should be near the club house. These two preliminary points settled, a bird's eye view of the ground from some eminence may probably suggest the positions for the other holes and teeing-grounds. . . .'

Then he gets down to detail.

> 'The first two or three holes should, if possible, be fairly long ones, and should be, comparatively speaking easy to play. Holes of a good length permit the players to get away without congesting the links, or, in the words of a Musselburgh caddie, it allows them to "get squandered". . . .
> . . . there should be at least two short holes within the reach of a good player with one stroke; these should be certain three's. . . .
>
> On new greens which are of a rough nature, the holes should be made shorter to begin with, until the ground is walked down. . . .
>
> The tees should be placed on level parts of the course with, if anything, a slight slope upwards in the direction to be played. . . .

The selection of putting-greens is a much more difficult matter. They may be on the level course, or in a natural hollow or basin, provided it be sufficiently large and shallow, or they may be placed on the tops of large "tables". All of these are good positions, and the more *variety* that can be introduced the better.

The putting greens should be as large as possible; and while the ground should be comparatively level, it is not desirable that it would be perfectly flat . . . but . . . of a slightly undulating character. If natural putting greens cannot be made on the course as it stands, then they must be dug up and laid with suitable turf; but this should only be done *as a last resource*.'

Times have certainly changed. Next, he examines hazards.

'There should not be any hazard out of which the ball cannot be extricated at the loss of one stroke, and all hazards should be visible to the golfer . . . before playing his stroke.

Trees are never fair hazard if at all near the line of play as a well-hit shot may be completely spoiled by catching in the branches. An occasional wall or fence or stream of water or pond to be crossed cannot always be avoided, but I do not recommend the making of such hazards merely as hazards.

The placing of hazards is a matter of great difficulty, and their positions should be such that a golfer who is playing a good shot should never visit them. The positions should be varied. There should, for example, be at certain holes, hazards that must be carried, and should be carried, from the tee . . . . At other holes the hazards should be placed so as to punish badly played second strokes; at others, again, the hazards should guard the putting-greens in front, and there may also be some hazards placed behind the greens.

Although blind holes (i.e. holes at which the player does not see the flag) are objectionable, they cannot always be dispensed with; but an endeavour should be made to place the hole in such a position that it can be seen in playing the approach.'

There is much more and a good deal of practical advice about changing holes and tee markers. But his whole attitude to design required acceptance of natural contours. He gave no advice (and indeed at that time it was hardly thinkable) on moulding land and producing artificial contours. And yet the landscape architects of a century before had known all about that. Golf course architecture was still purely an attribute of the game and of the land employed. It had no superior existence or notion of beauty in itself. Nevertheless by the turn of the century (or before or after depending on the age of the club and whether it was inland or at the sea), the early cruel hazards had often been tidied up. The old philosophy was weakening, or rather, emphasis was shifting. And now, we find a few names to conjure with. After golfing for thirty or forty years, leading players were beginning to analyse the elements they found most desirable in golf. The first of these was Garden G. Smith, the younger of two brothers who founded the Aberdeen University Golf Club in December 1878. Amongst other pursuits, he became editor of *Golf, Illustrated* which still flourishes. His book *The World of Golf* (1898), contains history, descriptions, travel and one chapter on 'The making and keeping of golf courses.' What he has to say is still eminently quotable though like some of his contemporaries, his attitude to bunkers is no longer fashionable. Much of what he says echoes the words of Willie Park so we will only repeat those views where he seems to have other or more developed ideas.

'Laying out a golf course is not a mathematical puzzle, and the position of the holes is to be settled by their suitability for the game, and not by the application of the Rule of Three.

To make a beginning, select a point for your club-house – close to which your first tee will inevitably be placed – which is as near as possible, either to the majority of the golfers' residences, or to the station, ...

Suppose there is a spot 300 yards away from your prospective club-house, either in a hollow or on a plateau, or in some other interesting situation, guarded by a bunker or other hazard, and which would make an excellent putting green, let not your soul be dismayed by the fact that to get there you have to walk through a perfect jungle of gorse. As a general principle, except on the putting green where it brings its own reward, a bad shot should be followed by a bad lie, and a good shot should be correspondingly rewarded by a good one. Now it is impossible, at every hole, to provide a fitting punishment for every kind of bad shot. But there is one kind of bad stroke which by universal consent must be summarily punished, whenever and wherever it is perpetrated, and that is a "topped shot". . . . Wherefore, in making your first tee, select a spot some sixty yards in front of which a yawning bunker stretches right across the course, and if it be so narrow, or so shallow, that a topped ball will jump over it or run through it, dig it wider and deeper, so that all balls crossing its jaws will inevitably be swallowed up. If no bunker is to be had, a pond will do equally well, or a railway or a hedge, or a wall – anything, in short, that is impassable.'

He evidently believed in an early knockout. But it is surprising how generally the following advice took root and survived even into the Fifties.

'A long driver, when he hits his ball clean, will carry some 150 to 170 yards, and a less powerful player some 130 to 150 yards. From 100 to 130 yards, then, from the tee, there should be another hazard of some sort to catch balls which, though good enough to escape the primal punishment for topped balls, have yet been hit with considerable inaccuracy. Beyond this second hazard the ground should be good for 80 or 100 yards, but guarding the hole again, there should be another hazard which the player will have to loft over before reaching the putting green. In addition, the course may be garnished on either side, according to the taste and fancy of the maker, with other hazards, to catch crooked balls, and also beyond the hole, to punish those that are hit too strongly, but "blind hazards", i.e., hazards which are not visible to the player, such as sunk ditches or holes, should either be rendered visible or filled up.

It is becoming the fashion . . . to make the carry for the tee shot so long, that only the longest drivers can accomplish it – that is to say, from 140 to 180 yards. . . . Against a strong wind, such carries are often impracticable, and they tend to develop a propensity to mere slogging, to the neglect of direction or accuracy, *altogether away from the traditions of the game.* If two players drive their balls equally truly from the tee, and one, by reason of strength, gets his 30 yards further than the other, the fact that he is 30 yards nearer the hole than his weaker brother, is surely a sufficient reward for his superiority.'

It all sounds very simple, and his next suggestion has certainly come back into vogue.

'A short hole should always be of a sporting character, whether it be surrounded by bunkers, its green but a small oasis in the middle of a Sahara, or if the way to it be so narrow, that only the straightest shot will escape destruction.'

His advice on tees is very much fuller than that of Willie Park.

'The teeing grounds for each hole are important items. Judging from those that are to be found in many places, it seems to be thought that any place will do, provided you stick two white discs in it, to mark it off. This is a grievous error, and the teeing ground should have the care and attention of the green-maker and keeper, as much as the putting greens. The first thing to be looked to in a teeing ground is its situation. It must not be so near the hole that parties playing from it, will interfere, in the slightest degree, with those playing to the previous hole. Nor should it, on the other hand, be so far away from the hole previously played, that players have to walk a hundred yards or so before reaching it. There is usually some spot, 30 or 40 yards to one side or other of the last green, from which it will be possible to strike tee shots with safety and if the ground be unsuitable, a proper teeing ground will have to be made. Ground that is on any kind of slope, unless it be slightly sloped upwards, is unsuitable for a teeing ground. The surface ought to be dead level, and if one has to be made, let it be at least 6 yards wide and as many deep. This will give plenty of room for constant changing of all the discs and resting the green.

In making teeing grounds, see that they are placed absolutely at right angles to the line for the hole; and that the discs are also always placed at the same angle. Nothing is more disconcerting, or fatal to accuracy, than neglect in this particular.

The extent of ground necessary for a putting green depends on its situation. If it be on a plateau, 30 or 40 yards all round the hole is none too much; if it lie in a hollow or basin a much smaller superficial area will suffice. In any circumstances, it ought to be of such a size, that a ball played on to it from a distance will have a reasonable chance of stopping on it.

Many greens are now well supplied with water, which has been done by the sinking of Artesian wells. This is a very costly arrangement, and the results of artificial watering are doubtful.'

He continues with a good deal more solid advice on the upkeep of the golf course from which we must prise this pearl:

'Roughly speaking, the distinguishing features of inland or park golf are trees and worms . . . . The tree is not and never has been . . . a golfing hazard. Bunkers . . . have always been on the ground and not suspended in mid-air.

With the worm it is different, he dieth not. . . .'

Lastly he turns to a few aspects of construction and the statement quoted at the beginning of our later chapter on Design, which we have been hearing in various forms ever since. His notion of hazards was so uncompromising that it must be quoted in full.

'The question of hazards on an inland course is an extremely difficult one. Sand bunkers of the orthodox kind are necessarily unobtainable, gorse is rare, and hedges and ditches, of more or less unnegotiable character, are their only substitutes. It is usually necessary, therefore, to make artificial hazards, and care must be taken, that these are made and placed with due regard to fairness, interest, and variety. And here let it be said, that whatever the nature of the hazard may be, be it a natural seaside bunker, or an inland hedge or ditch, or a patch of gorse, let there be no doubt as to where the hazard begins, or where it ends. If your bunker tapers off indistinctly into the fair green, cut it square, and to preserve its integrity, build round its face with wood or wattles. If your whins are patchy, and you grudge destroying the stragglers, enclose them all with a white chalk line or a little trench, and let all ground within the mark be 'hazard'. For an inland course, the only good kind of artificial hazard is made by digging a trench some six feet broad and about a foot deep, at the required place, and at a suitable angle to the line of the hole. The contents of this trench are built up, cop-wise, to the height of about three feet on its far side, and the embankment is turfed over. This opposing face should not be perpendicular, but should slope away at an angle, so as to give a player a chance of playing forward, over it, even if his ball lies close to the face. Wherever it is possible, the trench should be filled with some inches of sea-sand or gravel, and if this cannot be procured, cinders or ashes may be used as a substitute.

But whatever the composition of the bottom of the trench may be, it should not be allowed to become hard or caked, and should always be of a soft and yielding nature. But do not be in a hurry to cut and carve the turf of your inland course with bunkers and made tees. Where the ground is park-like, and devoid of natural hazards, it is wiser to experiment with wattles or hurdles, at various distances, until by experience of the course in all states of the wind, you are satisfied of the correct position for your hazards. If this is done, much labour and expense will be avoided.'

So the construction at an inland course was seen as anything but a landscaping exercise. Even the trees were a nuisance and had to go. Worms also were a nuisance but they survived for a few more years.

It might be thought extraordinary that so many excellent golf courses developed at a time when few if any people were specifically engaged in designing them, were it not for the total acceptance of natural forms and the role these play in the enjoyment of the game.

The links prototype was the product of fortuitous circumstances but there is still a real feeling that the more we reveal those features which echo traditional golf, the more likely we are to develop the site's full merits. Coupled with the implication that a golf course architect, wherever possible, is doing no more than unlock the treasure chest which Mother Nature has provided (Vanbrugh's 'midwife'), we have nevertheless noted a modifying influence exerted by the desire for better playing conditions where the chest contained too many ruts and rushes.

Within four years, J.H. Taylor in *Taylor on Golf* (1902) was laying down the law with the authority due from the first three of his five Open Championships. Five of the 41 chapters deal with matters of golf course architecture, but I will only quote briefly to show how his attitude was milder than the foregoing.

For the one-stroke hole; he thought 140–150 yards would be best even though a strong driver might get his ball 180 to 200 yards from the tee.

For the 2-stroke hole he suggested 320–330 taking 170 to 180 as a reasonable limit for the drive. He did not agree with the reasoning of those that put forward 380–400.

The 3-stroke hole seemed to him the simplest on which authorities might agree on the proper length. 470 yards could not be improved upon.

He was evidently no believer, as he later affirms, in 'slogger's golf'. The tendency to lengthen courses would not, he thought, be approved by the majority. Nor did he like holes cut in tricky and awkward positions. Altogether a kindly and gentle view of the game and support for its less competent players. But he was a gentle and kindly man, except when he wanted to win a tournament and the cap was pulled down and the jaw thrust out.

John Low's book *Concerning Golf* appeared in 1903. He was a St Andrews member, Captain of the Cambridge team and later edited Nesbit's *Golf Yearbook*. Chapter IX was headed 'The Links'. After stressing the benefits of the infinite variety between golf links, he develops the theme:

'Every fresh hole we play should teach us some new possibility of using our strokes and suggest to us a further step in the progress of our golfing knowledge. Inland golf is often decried, and is certainly not so pleasant as the seaside game, but it is a splendid schooling as a supplement to the more sterling stuff. Most of the finest players of to-day have played much of their golf on inland greens, and have learned that the shots which are necessary on such links are often expedient on the classical courses. The very worst greens often teach us the most, even as the worst lies when overcome make us the more master of every possibility of situation.'

He would find less support for the last comment today; certainly not amongst the professionals and especially not from that admirable American tournament player who, when fined $100 for calling the course a 'cow pasture', wrote out a cheque for $200 because, he said, he intended to say exactly the same thing next day.

Next, Low defines a good test of golf:

'A course which necessitates power combined with great accuracy on the part of the player supplies the first principles of a good test . . . the course which requires, in addition to those things, the playing of the greatest variety of strokes, will be the best test of all'.

He quotes St Andrews and Hoylake:

'The second holes at St Andrews and Hoylake illustrate what I mean. The first shot must be played well to the right in both cases, in order to get to the best position from which to conduct further operations. The playing of the hole thus becomes not a series of isolated shots with no bearing the one on the others, but each stroke has to be played in relation to the following one, and the hole mastered by a pre-conceived plan of action.'

This is a classic conception, and after considering bunkering to give the skilful player the advantage over the slogger, he produces another:

'What tests good golf is the hazard which may or may not be risked; the bunker which takes charge of the long but not quite truly hit ball.'

And later:

'There is hardly such a thing as an unfair bunker. Even the hazard right in the middle of the course at the end of a long tee shot, like the ninth hole bunker at St Andrew's is really quite a fair risk.'

And another still:

'But golf need not be played in bee-lines. It is a mistake to suppose that because you hit a shot straight down the middle of the course and find it bunkered you are to fill up the offending hazard. Next time you will play on the true line, not on the bee-line, and all will be well. There seem to me to be far too few "round-the-corner" holes in golf.'

He sums up as follows:

'The greedy golfer will go too near and be sucked in to his destruction. The straight player will go just as near as he deems safe, just as close as he dare. Just as close as he dare: that's golf, and that's a hazard of immortal importance! For golf at its best should be a contest of risks. The fine player should . . . be just slipping past the bunkers, gaining every yard he can, conquering by the confidence of his own "far and sure" play. The less skilful player should wreck himself either by attempting risks which are beyond his skill, or by being compelled to lose ground through giving the bunkers a wide berth.'

He concludes that good bunkers, bunkers of strong character, refuse to be disregarded, and insist on asserting themselves: they do not mind being avoided, but they decline to be ignored.

On short holes, he also has useful comments which are certainly worthy of being recalled today.

'The short hole should not be long . . . many short holes are spoilt because of their length; and others that are not too long are not so good as they ought to be, because they require a blind shot. . . .

The short hole, if it requires a full drive, differs in no way, as far as the tee shot is concerned, from the longer holes, and does not supply that variety which constitutes its "raison d'être". The first point therefore we demand in a short hole is that it should be short enough to call from the player some judgement as to strength. . . .'

As to visibility:

'. . . joy cannot be ours unless we see the ground plan of our short hole from tee to flag, and can note the things which make or mar our hazard. The short hole should therefore be of debatable length, and the player should be able to see the spot on which he strives to pitch his ball.'

His peroration has a few words on length and then ends with a colourful climax:

'A perfect tee shot should make the following shot less difficult; a perfect second should only be probable after a perfect first. The heart of golf lies in propelling the ball accurately from one situation to another. Each step in the journey should be hazardous; the links should be almost too difficult for the player, bunkers should more perfectly abound.'

Apart from that last flight of fancy, it is a little humbling that after 75 years we have got nothing better to say on these matters. Perhaps it would be more humbling were there not the tremendous gulf between saying it and doing it.

H.S. Colt, who started his principal career about this time, thought much the same as Low but on the Eden Course at St Andrews (1914), although he was feeling his way into the landscape aspect of the job and did much to relieve the flatness of the site, he was not yet ready, or the money was lacking, or the machinery was lacking for the fully rounded realizations which came later. The golf course architect was ready to operate on favourable territory but not yet able to go it alone without Nature.

The same limitations applied to the professional golfers who, *faute de mieux*, were consulted about new courses. The gift of an eye for the land did not always match playing skill and Herbert Fowler, another 'amateur' was the next. He wrote in 1906 about how he tackled the job of making Walton Heath.

Having settled on the spots which he thought would make the most interesting greens and started clearing, he came down to detail. We see now a change of attitude to features not matching the classic pattern:

'There are, to be sure, all kinds of hazards, and most of them are bad: trees, hedges, ditches and all unsatisfactory, and no doubt the best are sand bunkers, so long as they are properly placed and constructed.'

He discussed cross hazards, side hazards, related hazards:

'Where you have a long hole it is, I think, a good plan to have a cross bunker to catch the topped second shot, and these hazards also tend to make players use their heads'. (Both Walton Heath 18th holes still confirm this belief.)

Personally, I think that a slice is certainly a greater fault than a top, and I would, therefore, place a majority of the side hazards on the right and a lesser number on the left of the fairway. Another point in favour of side hazards is that it is far more difficult to avoid a hazard than to carry one.

In placing bunkers . . . great attention should be paid to so arranging them that they should work in with the hazards in close proximity to the green. Thus, in a hole of say, 500 yards long, if a bunker is placed on the left-hand front corner of the green it will be seen that the nearer the player can pass the right-hand bunker the less the bunker in the green will affect his approach shot.

The ideal hole, of course, should have difficulties both in the tee and approach shots, and, if possible, the hazards should be so arranged that a player having "placed" his tee shot shall play the second shot at an advantage over the player who has been wild.

All greens are the better for side hazards of some sort or another, and personally I am in favour of hazards behind the green too, though they are not of such importance as those on the sides.'

As we have seen, many of these notions reflect the views of John Low but he goes a little further:

'There should, if possible, be an "entrance" to all greens. By this I do not mean two bunkers, placed with mathematical accuracy exactly opposite each other on the right and left corners of the green, but that there should be a definite entrance to play for. It answers quite well and *does not look so formal* if one bunker is some little distance in front of the green on one side, and another starts in the corner of the opposite side and takes a turn and runs some distance down the side of it. The width of the entrance should vary with the distance from which the approach shot has been played.'

Note that comment on placing side hazards at greens. Staggering them *does not look so formal*. Landscape effect has crept into the vocabulary for the first time.

In the same book, *Golf Greens and Greenkeeping* 1906, there is also a chapter by James Braid. He raises bunker banks *to make them look as natural as possible*. These are the first hints of moving away from making and planning greens and hazards for theoretical reasons only.

In 1908, James Braid followed on with *Advanced Golf* and devoted two chapters to very precise ideas on golf course architecture. To summarize the main points: every natural obstacle to be used

– complete variety of holes in length character, and design – always well guarded putting greens. The shorter the hole, the smaller the green. Alternative tees. Bunkering for positional play. Alternative routes.

This section ends with a bold comment: 'A course which conforms to all these general principles cannot possibly be a bad one'. One hopes so. Then he discusses individual yardages. Four short holes, all different: two very long holes, maximum 550, the rest 320 to 420, preferably above 360; two stiff carries; preference to side bunkering; balance between the halves, three longish holes to open; the last two or three holes all of good length; total length 6000 to 6400. On short holes, he too echoes J.L. Low: putting greens should be of all kinds, sizes and undulations though no. 18 might be flat to reduce luck. Bunkers should catch particular kinds of defective shots.

He is then first to recommend the diagonal style of bunkering and gives diagrams. He ends on the keynote: 'The more natural hazards there are on a course whatever their character, the more interesting that course ought to be, and generally is.'

Much of this seems to have been derived from Fowler but perhaps that is inevitable where both were contributors to the same book and fashion limited discussion to certain basic points. It was a question of who was first in print.

By now, therefore, there is some progress on design, though not much more on landscaping, although we have still got the natural hazards we started with. It is only proper to add that much of the merit of Braid's courses were derived from the construction work done by Stutt. As stated earlier, it is one thing to talk good architecture, it is another to do it. . . .

One other essay in the first decade, mostly on greenkeeping, was written by H.S. Colt (born 1869); a solicitor, secretary of Sunningdale, and finally a designer of great distinction over thirty years. His next essay was in *The Book of the Links* (1912). Clearly in the main stream, he too believed that the only way to make attractive land provide satisfactory golf was to work in all the natural features, not developing them more than was essential but using them fully to provide a course with its own character.

On planning, once the clubhouse location was fixed it was simple enough to fix Tee no. 1 with the 10th near at hand if possible. He liked two long holes to start the round and get players away, but after that he did not stipulate any particular sequence because what he wanted was variety and natural features produced that quality as well.

He did not approve of blind shots and thought length had very little to do with quality. He liked elasticity, that is to say walking forward to the next tee normally, but back for more length for special occasions. This was a new contribution to the discussion though most committees later tended to use the elastic for ordinary support. At the same time he liked a number of tees giving more variety by offering different angles to the fairway.

For related reasons he recommended the diagonal cross hazard as James Braid had done four years before.

There were also echoes of earlier writers near the green. He made his green entrances narrower than for the tee-shot, but never opposite each other, more at right angles to the line of play. He also introduces the third dimension into his thinking – little turf hollows drawing from the green, slopes and hillocks to give variety of the difficult stances and lies which make a great golf course. Indeed, he wanted variety in difficulties, variety in hazards and bunkers, avoidance of symmetry in artificial work. The landscape could be made 'still more pleasing to the eye' by irregular groups of gorse broom or tussocky grass, even small birch and pine trees.

His appreciation of the *genius loci* led him to select ridges, banks or hollows for bunkers and ridges or low plateaux for greens rather than hollows because he strove for visibility.

Finally, he disposed once and for all of any idea of regular dimensions for tees or greens. He was 'sick to death' of so many 'thirty by thirties in greens and ten by tens in tees'. Standardization destroyed half the joy of the game. The designer should see and use 'the natural features present on each course to the fullest possible extent'.

In the same year, Harry Vardon joined the other two members of the Great Triumvirate on the bookshelves with *How to Play Golf* (1912) the successor to his first book *The Complete Golfer*. This time he wrote a complete chapter on Golf Course Architecture. Nor was it relegated to the later pages. It appeared immediately after Chapter I 'The Trend of the Game' in which he has much of interest to say about the gutty against the Haskell. He even says that although he had won the Open Championship in 1911 and several other competitions 'the actual quality of my golf was four strokes a round worse than it was with the gutta percha ball.'

From a man with thoughts like that we can expect traditionalism in his golf course architecture and indeed he regrets that since the rubber-cored ball arrived, the great tendency had been to abandon cross hazards and replace them with bunkers and 'various other agents of retribution on the wings, with an occasional pot bunker towards the middle of the course'.

He wanted to restore the old standard of golf by reviving the cross bunker; not the dull, unnatural-looking type at right angles to play, but a diagonal design, the furthest part on the line to the hole. (Or a chain of three or four on the same angle.) The green should be long and narrow to match this scheme and angled only towards the direct line.

He wanted five holes of about 400 yards with a hazard to be carried 40 yards short of the green and four holes from 330–370 yards. Short holes should be well bunkered with one 80–120 yards; two, 120–160; and two for full shots. The remaining few holes should be 420–500. He did not think that any hole need run to 600 yards.

There is a good deal of advice on bunkering; for example, those guarding the back of the green should be 'at a respectful distance – say, from ten to fifteen yards beyond the hole'.

He believed that 'the course should be made to look *as natural as possible*'. The hazard's position is guided by knowledge of the game, but its contouring is a matter of *artistry*. Those level with the fairway with a bulwark of earth on the far side were not proper for the approach. The mounds which had become popular recently should resemble those of the originators at Mid-Surrey. He also liked undulating greens. But the chapter ends with another appeal to 'check the craze for the running shot'. Back to the cross hazard.

So just before the 1914–1918 War we have not only sentences but whole paragraphs devoted to landscaping and even some advice on choice of situation to make a happy landscape effect more likely.

All this then was taken up and developed vigorously by Dr Alistair Mackenzie who was Colt's partner in 1920 when he wrote *Golf Architecture*. He produced 13 points for the Ideal Golf Course. Many of them echo not only the ideas but the words of his master.

1. Two loops of nine holes are preferable.
2. At least four short holes, two or three drive and pitch holes and a large preponderance of good two shot holes.
3. Short walks only from green to following tee, preferably forward to leave elasticity for future lengthening.
4. Undulating greens and fairways but no hill climbing.
5. A different character to every hole.
6. Minimum blindness for the approach.
7. Beautiful surroundings and man-made features, indistinguishable from Nature.
8. Sufficient heroic carries from the tee but alternative routes for the shorter player if he sacrifices a stroke or half a stroke.
9. Endless variety in shot making.
10. No lost balls.
11. Playing interest to stimulate improvement in performance.
12. High scoring golfers should still be able to enjoy the layout.
13. Perfect greens and fairways, approaches equal to greens and conditions just as good in winter as in summer.

If we analyse this programme we find it is not all golf course architecture, because the thirteen points divide up very roughly like this:

{ Planning }	1, 2, 3, 6, 12	=	5 }
{ Design }	4, 5, 7, 8, 9	=	5 }
Greenkeeping	10, 13	=	2
Psychological	11	=	1

He went on to interpret this programme all over the world while Colt took on C.H. Alison to assist him abroad and John Morrison at home.

There have been plenty of later practitioners but they have not been able to uncover much basically new philosophy beyond that set out from Park to Mackenzie. It is, indeed, surprising that within the small space of 25 years, a complete dossier on bunkering, tees, greens, layout and construction had been assembled, some of it derivative, some recognizing opposing points of view, especially in respect of rough and trees, which still remain contentious. It is even more surprising that the far greater number of later practitioners have not uncovered any truly original thinking on the art, but merely put on the old play in modern dress.

This quarter century also contained five years of war when golf courses, competitive golf and so many of the original golfing brotherhood were lost. Moreover, in 1902 the Haskell ball was introduced though this must have been far less revolutionary than the introduction of the 'gutty' in 1848.

The other singular feature of these formative years is the early acceptance of an aesthetic approach undeveloped by any previous landscape experience or study. Here were men trained in pro's shop, law, doctoring, and administration applying the imitation of Nature to their artificial construction as if they were the first to discover it.

They were not always successful. There was a sense in which the early choice of heath, pine forest and common land for the first inland courses conceded contours some of which would not altogether be approved today. Such land had frequently been superficially shaped by ancient encampments, gravel workings and military exercises and these random excavations and embankments crept into design in the earliest days. Moreover, the associated maintenance problems were less apparent on poor soil. But above all the links prototype contained gradients, acceptable aesthetically and in adventurous golf, which our thinking, perhaps wrongly, has eliminated in favour of the suave, apparently endless grading of the scraper.

We have tagged along behind the techniques of earth moving to the point where there is a danger of imposing a standard concept on every site by sheer technical skill. I hope that this review of the philosophy from which we have developed should help us to keep our feet on the ground in every sense of the words.

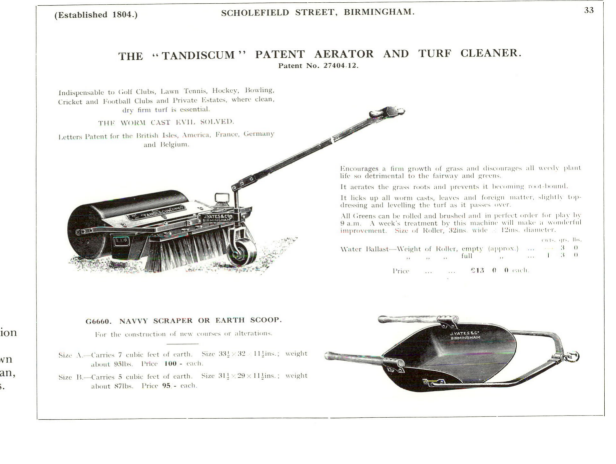

Fig. 2.3   Before the combustion
engine was applied to earth
moving, the earth scoop, drawn
by a horse and guided by a man,
was used for contour changes.
(Courtesy of J. Yates & Co.,
Birmingham.)

THE "TANDISCUM" PATENT AERATOR AND TURF CLEANER.
Patent No. 27404·12.

Indispensable to Golf Clubs, Lawn Tennis, Hockey, Bowling,
Cricket and Football Clubs and Private Estates, where clean,
dry firm turf is essential.

THE WORM CAST EVIL SOLVED.

Letters Patent for the British Isles, America, France, Germany
and Belgium.

Encourages a firm growth of grass and discourages all weedy plant
life so detrimental to the fairway and greens.

It aerates the grass roots and prevents it becoming root-bound.

It licks up all worm casts, leaves and foreign matter, slightly top-
dressing and levelling the turf as it passes over.

All Greens can be rolled and brushed and in perfect order for play by
9 a.m.   A week's treatment by this machine will make a wonderful
improvement.   Size of Roller, 32ins. wide × 12ins. diameter.

                                                          cwts. qrs. lbs.
Water Ballast—Weight of Roller, empty (approx.) ...   3   0
        „   „   „   full   ...   1   3   0

              Price   ...   ...   £13 0 0 each.

G6660. NAVVY SCRAPER OR EARTH SCOOP.

For the construction of new courses or alterations.

Size A.—Carries 7 cubic feet of earth.   Size 33½×32×11½ins.; weight
        about 93lbs.   Price 100/- each.

Size B.—Carries 5 cubic feet of earth.   Size 31½×29×11½ins.; weight
        about 87lbs.   Price 95/- each.

If we unlock the genius of the place, we shall ensure the variety, interest and enjoyment which, lacking our resources the earliest golf course architects achieved hand in hand with Nature herself.

2.2 THE MIDDLE AGE

Early planning was therefore as much dominated by the character of the site itself as the original unplanned courses. Between the wars, there was only a little movement away from this relationship. Tom Simpson, the most vocal of practitioners (than whom nobody could better model a green), called this era 'The Golden Age'. He singled out the artificial Victorian style of construction and the design usually associated with it which he called 'penal'. This epithet has been quoted and illustrated ever since. But the 'gun platform' and 'Bechers Brook' type of green and bunker occupied only a small part of the total development of the game in small pockets and they are of only passing significance. There is so little precise science in basic golf course architecture, that this simple distinction between penal and strategic is often inflated beyond its importance. One may also overlook the often suburban nature of the boom in the first thirty years of this century. This inevitably restricted land area. 18 holes were often packed into 100 acres or less. This could only be achieved by planning a large proportion of nearly parallel holes. If holes are mostly parallel there is only room to sketch in strategic qualities and they may be so subtle as to be barely distinguishable from James Braid's slice and hook bunkering. Truly strategic design requires considerable elbow room. Hence one element in the greater popularity of courses built further out in Surrey or Berkshire where the ultimate bliss of holes totally separated from each other could also be realized. A golf course architect is no better than the site he is given though he may be better within that framework than his peers.

Simpson was a stimulating and often controversial exponent of the art. Henry Longhurst, writing of him soon after Simpson's death, said that nobody had suffered more than he from retrograde changes to his work. He pushed design to the limit and beyond it occasionally but the basic excellence and beauty of courses like Spa, Liège, and Royal Antwerp in Belgium, Morfontaine and

Hardelot in France, certainly proclaim a master hand. Part at least of this success must have been due to his skill as a draughtsman. He was also the first, so far as I know, to use a surveyors' level. The work was getting more technical, although boning rods still survived. He left less to the contractor than anyone before him and could precisely describe and draw what he wanted. It is worth quoting him at some length to see the original thoughts he added. *The Architectural Side of Golf* (1929) with H.N. Wethered was his first treatise. It is a beautiful book in itself and contains the excellent sketches which Simpson provided on his individual hole plans to illustrate green and approach modelling. Only 43 pages are devoted to golf course architecture as such, but they echo

(a)   (b)

Fig. 2.4   Two examples of my father's 1920s bunkering. (a) The 15th green at Lickey Hills, Birmingham. (b) The Bassett layout at Southampton.

and amplify the views of his predecessors and are set out more provocatively. He sees the job of the golf course architect as defence against the attack of new skills, clubs and golf balls. But that defence should be by no means passive.

He quotes an article in The Field concerning the 4th hole at Woking. According to Darwin (Bernard) there was a discussion about the central fairway bunker at this hole at a Green Committee meeting. Simpson went out alone afterwards to contemplate it. What he saw interested him so much that he decided to become a golf course architect himself.

When he discusses the role of the golf course architect he is more subtle than his predecessors. He would not make too obvious the correct interpretation of a hole but only the intelligent golfer would uncover it. He would not deliberately conceal it but he was certainly prepared to lay false scents. This was something fresh and stimulating – a few cobwebs could be dusted away.

I cannot say to what extent the new ideas belonged to Simpson or to Wethered or, as is probable, to both. Simpson was a barrister although he never practised and therefore likely to have been more willing to expound his theories as he did in subsequent essays and to green committees in uncompromising reports. Henry Longhurst recalled that while one committee was deliberating, Simpson drove round and round the clubhouse in his Rolls Royce. The point or humour of this performance is difficult to unravel but it is perhaps indicative of a teasing attitude to life which found substance in his designs. His beret, shooting stick and cloak were in the same vein.

But the greens he designed have never been bettered and he gives one of those sets of rules which made the task look deceptively simple.

1. Avoid balance.
2. Visible green surface at short holes, but complete visibility not essential at those over 400 yards where the target is the flag stick not the hole.
3. Large flat greens negate scientific and artistic design.
4. Greens should never be quite round or square. A pear shape is more desirable generally.
5. Remember the greenkeeper's cutting and hole-changing requirements. Make enough flat areas to provide a 6 feet circle round hole positions. Three quarters of the putting surface should be flat.

6. Two levels separated by a low mound are very acceptable, but outline and area will vary according to the range and position of the approach shot.
7. Artificial green construction should be avoided unless absolutely necessary. Then make sure it looks like original ground.
8. Differentiate greens on one course. Resist copying famous models but by all means use some of their principal features.
9. Entrance to greens at holes:
    375–475 yards – about 20 yards
    325–375 yards – about 18 yards, both being modified by 'gather' on the approach. Fix the centre then view it from the approach shot to fix the inner ends of wing bunkers.
10. Avoid excessive undulations and allow a player to gauge line and strength reasonably accurately.
11. Green bunkers should only exceed three exceptionally.

He was one of the first to play that eclectic game which is popular with golfing journalists in winter or used to be before the Sunshine Circuit took them away from home in January and February.

Simpson's choice was as follows, with metric measurements added for comparison:

		Yards	*Metres*
1.	Hoylake no. 1	440	402
2.	West Hill no. 15	175	160
3.	Walton Heath Old no. 17	460	421
4.	Addington New no. 8	380	347
5.	Westward Ho. no. 5	160	146
6.	Worplesdon no. 11	520	475
7.	Turnberry New no. 16	350	320
8.	Hoylake no. 7	200	183
9.	St Andrews no. 14	527	482
		3212	2936

		Yards	*Metres*
10.	Prestwick no. 17	383	350
11.	Westward Ho! no. 16	138	126
12.	Royal St George's no. 15	457	418
13.	Liphook no. 14	420	384
14.	Sunningdale Old no. 12	400	366
15.	St Andrews no. 17	456	417
16.	Rye no. 8	165	151
17.	Saunton no. 17	440	402
18.	Muirfield no. 9	475	434
		3334	3048
		3212	2936
		6546	5984

This is rather longer than he generally considered adequate, i.e. about 6350 yards. It is probably no accident that all except two are on sand of some sort and the two exceptions are on gravel.

Not all these have survived and others have changed. The cruellest loss of all was the New Course at Addington after the 1939–1945 war. (J.F. Abercromby at his best.)

In this period, besides the firm of Colt, Alison, Morrison already mentioned, the three Majors, C.K. Hutchison, Guy Campbell and S.V. Hotchkin, M.C., did a good deal of work. Hutchison helped James Braid at Gleneagles, Guy Campbell, another Etonian, was involved at West Sussex (Pulborough), at Killarney, Skegness, Rye, and Trevose. Colonel Hotchkin, as he became, felt that too much of the responsibilities of the partnership devolved on him at Pulborough and went off to make several fine courses in South Africa, Humewood being probably the finest, and its 13th hole, outstanding. He also completely remodelled Macauvlei where he used to disappear into the bush with sandwiches for hours on end. He is best remembered in the UK for the perfection he brought to Woodhall Spa. Leeds Castle is another gem. He wrote a number of articles which were collected into a booklet by the editor of *Club Sportsman* in which they first appeared. Some of the headings will illustrate his approach: 'Architect and Artist: Studying Nature; the A & B Solution; the Green governs play'. But he also dealt with implements, greenkeeping operations and even buying a tractor. It is interesting that a man of action, after a career including 21st Lancers, the Leicestershire Yeomanry, Lindsey County Council and the House of Commons, found such evident satisfaction in this creative urge for golf courses. They could not have been so good without a high degree of dedication.

Guy Campbell also gave up the 'Major' when he succeeded to the baronetcy. He wrote *Golf for Beginners* in 1923 and devoted the eight pages of Chapter VI to diagrams and a swift *tour d'horizon* of building a golf course. Make use of all natural hazards but avoid trees. Avoid built up teeing grounds. *Never* build high plateau greens. On manures: use as little as possible and then in the Spring. Weeding: do it by hand. All very terse and circumscribed. But he later practised what he preached in Britain, USA and France where he is reputed to have driven in a vintage Rolls Royce. On the back seat was a cage and in the cage was a parrot.

2.3   TRANSITION

That period from 1920–1930 while one of great development in the number of courses (fifty a year in the UK) still did not produce any startling departure from the theories of golf course planning and design already established: nor, indeed, has any subsequent decade though fashions have come and gone. The repertoire is deceptively simple – so simple that the inexperienced are still inclined to attempt it in spite of the portents. The old construction techniques were equally simple – thirty or forty men with spades and wheelbarrows, the horse and scoop and, later, the Allan Taylor and the Pattisson tractors. The Ruston-Bucyrus excavator was also used, but earth movement on a big scale was seldom contemplated.

The game itself had settled into a recognizable comfortable pattern. Professionals spent their winters at their clubs as they did their summers between tournaments. These events were friendly affairs generally sponsored by newspapers and golf ball manufacturers. The leading amateurs were mostly those with the most leisure. There were a few practice grounds, but they figured far less in

Contractors to
ROYAL AIR FORCE and
Hundreds of other Golf Clubs.

The 1931 A.T. Golf Tractor.

Prices of different Models range from £110 to £225.   All Models can be fitted with the A.T. Water Pump.

ALLAN-TAYLOR ENGINEERING & MANUFACTURING CO., 118-128 HIGH ST., WANDSWORTH, S.W.18.

Fig. 2.5   Everybody's tractor in the '30s, built on a cut-down Ford chassis. The Pattison tractor was similar.

the scheme of things than today. As a result, the Open Championship was won by an American from 1924 to 1933 until Henry Cotton had conceived the desire to win and taken steps to do so.

After 1945 that kind of dedication became universally accepted as indeed it has in all other sports. Judgement of distance or estimation of hole position was replaced by pocket charts defining both, while precision was equally demanded of swings, clubs, golf balls and playing surfaces.

Design was obliged to react again and for the first time there were regularly playing lengths exceeding 7000 yards. There was a fashion for big greens because greens had to be big if enough target areas suitably defined by rolling contours were to be provided. Tees grew enormously.

But the art was now assisted by earth-moving capabilities which turned the old approach to natural feature upside down. Instead of using what natural feature the site possessed, the site could now be endowed with whatever natural feature the architect fancied. A lot of them fancied water. Lakes on flat Florida sites were readily constructed and conveniently provided the fill for the elevation and modelling of greens, tees and bunkers.

However, Man is not yet all that superior to Nature being, fortunately, a very small part of it, and this move away from the genius of the site has led to a style which, however beautiful in itself (and many such courses are undeniably beautiful and good), tends to be repetitive on the surface at least. The make-up is too heavy, the lips and cheeks too red, the eyes too brilliant. A moment's inattention on the Costa del Golf and one can forget which seductive golf course one is courting.

This similarity has led later designers to seek the bizarre or outré to stamp their own inimitable seal on their creations. Unfortunately eccentrics are all too easily imitable and become a model for the less talented. Railway sleepers have reappeared here and there, quite irrationally and not always properly as sleepers but as logs set on end supporting a face so shallow that there is really no need to support it. This is a landscape gardening trick not meant for golf. Greens totally surrounded by sand or water have also crept into some vernaculars. The only way we can go from here is back. Fortunately, there are plenty of golf course architects who see a future only in shorter, more natural courses and smaller greens, even in the USA. Let us hope that developers will see it the same way.

Golf course architecture, given the simplicity of its theory, has in many ways become an exercise in pure landscaping. Horatio Brown, Humphrey Repton, and Uvedale Price would have been the Trent Jones of their time if golf had started its growth that much earlier. One American golf course architect of some distinction not only has never played golf, but also actively denies the desirability of his doing so. Another, much younger, exercises his protest against the trends of modern golf and, presumably, golf course architecture in the USA by playing with hickory shafts.

One may also suspect an over-reaction in design and preparation of surfaces to improved playing skills, concentrating attention too precisely on the small group at the top. This may make the

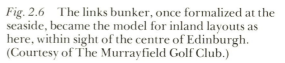

Fig. 2.6 The links bunker, once formalized at the seaside, became the model for inland layouts as here, within sight of the centre of Edinburgh. (Courtesy of The Murrayfield Golf Club.)

leaders score better, if there is any sense in which good design inspires good play and poor design is only frustrating. Such concentration, nevertheless, seems to spread the field out more widely. It improves a few, but has the opposite effect on others who score erratically with differences between rounds of as much as twenty shots. Perhaps they are playing for fun. Let us hope they are having some.

However, for most of us, the need to make judgements at the highest level is rare and life on the developing fringe will always be controversial. What is more interesting for present purposes is the steadfast refusal of the bulk of golfers to return lower scores because of a new set of clubs, or to hit the ball further because of high compression or wafer-thin covers. If there is any doubt about how difficult to make a course for the scratch golfer, there is none whatever about the need to provide latitude for those with handicaps.

Fortunately, in dealing with a variety of skills, golf course architecture presents no dilemma. It is founded on options as John L. Low first pointed out. A golf course in principle can only be planned and designed to the standard of scratch because that is the only standard which is predictable and that is also the standard which all golfers will achieve at occasional holes: a handicap represents the inability to do so repeatedly, not necessarily the difficulty of the course. However, if the hole is difficult on the scratch route, the provision of alternative lines and forward tees will be equitable and appropriate.

In the Thirties it became fashionable to set markers on the edge of fairways at 200 yards. (Post-war, one club even defined distances from the green.) This caused the authorities to forbid the practice, but not the early morning pacing for professional caddies prior to a tournament. To pass the 200 yard marker in 1939 was, for the middle handicap golfer, very satisfactory; 230 yards seemed to be the ultimate goal. Those who could comfortably hit that distance in those days would, other things being equal, achieve 250 and more today. But the majority are still back where their fathers and grandfathers would have been in 1939.

Appendix 1 shows a table prepared for the British Association of Golf Course Architects by Golf Course Measurements Ltd, which illustrates the passive resistance of Mr Average Golfer to the blandishments of magazines, advertising or tutors.

In *The Glorious World of Golf* (1973) Peter Dobereiner quotes A.A. Milne's comment 'Golf is the best game in the world at which to be bad'. While there are many who need the stimulus of increasing skill if their interest is to be maintained, the pleasures of simply playing at any level of the game are so strong that they retain the allegiance of millions of 'no hopers'. It is, however, unfortunate that one of the ways in which such do hope to play better is by long, reflective assessments of lie, line and weather prior to sundry practice swings, some of which remove additional pieces of turf. The sadness of failure after all this preparation must be much more acute than any regrets over a shot missed quickly.

The same kind of sadness often occurs after the first round over a new hotel or development golf course which has been preceded by publicity write-ups which will undoubtedly have described the new gem as exciting and unique. These overtempting hors d'oeuvres stimulate the appetite beyond the point where the meagre diet which follows can satisfy it.

Apart from classic successes like Muirfield, one of the few golf courses where realization lives up to and even exceeds expectation is Pine Valley, New Jersey. In that case the publicity has not been contrived but self-generating. Indeed with its old-fashioned stress on difficulty it is even off-putting. But the fact is a beautifully tended, romantic layout difficult indeed and even very slightly suspect in some of its green formations but unexpectedly beautiful, dramatic and inspiring: even (perhaps one can safely use the word at last) unique. And it was finished in 1920.

2.4 LESSONS

The changes in golf course architecture have therefore been primarily matters of degree as numbers, skills, constructional techniques, and implements have improved. If we can understand this simple relationship we shall be better able to determine our own job in reflecting the needs of today's players while continuing the traditions which have survived the past.

Firstly, the length of courses. We have seen that it started to increase quite early in the piece and is still doing so. Quite illogically, a hole is still often thought to be better because it is longer – a course is thought to be superior at 6800 yards to one of 6500. If the object of the game were to

Fig. 2.7 Classic simplicity, post-war. The 6th at Turnberry, Scotland. Mackenzie Ross. (W. Neale, Action Photos.)

hit the ball further than the next man, there would be merit in that point of view, but the best design encourages thought and choice rather than indiscriminate hitting and all the early writers agreed that this was the gospel.

Equally, repeated demands for long irons and wooden club shots will be less agreeable than calling for a variety of approaches. On some sites, repetition will become downright boring. Unless, therefore, we are operating for speculators who need or believe they need extreme length for publicity purposes, let us restrict any desire to follow this trend automatically. It may be true that a particular hole would be improved by the addition of a tee adding 20 yards. But that will depend on a variety of factors which will be affected by length, but never on length itself.

Secondly, the promoters of travel and tourism through golf have taken a large number of club golfers to various Spanish Costas, where they can live and golf for a week or two on luxurious urbanizations with rolling fairways, studded with palm trees and impeccable, velvety greens. The exercise is beneficial to their health so long as the next round of golf on their native Sludgecombe Valley does not produce nostalgia. This feeling is apt to be followed by jaded comments on bunkers, greens, tees, the standard of upkeep, the greenkeeper and the Green Committee. A month or so earlier the same player might have been saying that the greens were 'putting very well' and the course was 'coming on nicely'. He has made false comparisons. The two types of course are on parallel lines which never meet. It would be unwise to try suddenly to bend the direction which the native product has taken over fifty years or more; and even more so, to ask members to pay the bill.

Thirdly, with the increase in the number of players, the safety standards acceptable in the past are often inadequate today. Some, regrettably, are also less patient than their fathers. At any rate their fathers like to think so. Coupled with these factors, injured citizens are apt to be more litigious and the potential seriousness of accidents which can occur has greatly increased. A country road may have become a trunk route with motor-coaches passing regularly; a belt of trees may now contain gardens where children play. While these risks may be insurable, it is better to avoid them. Many suggestions for the improvement of existing holes involve a reduction of safety margins. In one sense this should be the first thing to be verified because it is unlikely that much useful space is still wasted in a layout of considerable age. Its potential will have been realized and employed long since. Most proposals for major changes of layout will involve the safety factor. A modification which increases danger has not even got the excuse, which many danger points may plead, that it has been there a long time. And, indeed, a long acquaintanceship with old hazards will often have led to a mutual respect between golfers and passers-by which overcomes a problem whereas a new one will provide anger and confrontation. Granny Clark's Wynd, across nos 1 and 18, is not ideally situated at St Andrews, but has become part of the fabric of the course and the townspeople who happen not to be playing golf do not inconvenience those that are. It is also a One Way Street. This is very different from the situation which can arise today if proposals to play close to roads or footpaths are implemented. It is fortunate that few accidents seem to occur even in dangerous situations. But they can be serious or even fatal when they do.

Fourthly, as we shall see later, the increased traffic on golf courses leads to increased wear on areas unable to support it. Changes and plans which tend to disperse traffic should be preferred to those which concentrate it. Every new tee or green bunker should be studied from this point of view so that flow round the course will not be disturbed and so that players moving between holes will not disturb others in play.

But those are mostly practical matters. Do we not need to establish some doctrine which can guide us to the light? The man with a feeling for the history of the game can certainly argue the merits of holes by analogy, by tradition, by common consent, and by their survival. That seems to be a good start. He should also be able to recognize the factors which lead to enjoyment. For over fifty years I have never heard any words but praise for a day's golf at the West Sussex Golf Club at Pulborough (so much so that I have never dared to go there in case this perfect image were damaged). I take this to mean that the approach, the site, the view, the layout, the design, the maintenance, the locker room, the bar, the staff, and the luncheon are all about right. Perhaps we tend to forget the importance of the *total* experience and concentrate too much on the detail of the course, though it is precisely the tiny detail which may control the decision taken on any particular shot. But at least we can be sure that if the course is right, the scene is set for everything else to fall into place. How do we ensure that the course is absolutely right?

That seems to be a long laborious job but at least most of it should be over by now. The original

Fig. 2.8 No. 12 green, Mortonhall, Edinburgh, lies on a strong slope away from the approach. Build-up was reduced by limiting front to back measurement and by slight 'cut' at the front edge. (Courtesy of S.R. Jamieson, Edinburgh.)

planning, design and construction processes will, we hope, have produced a satisfactory golf course. But there is so much going on at once, over a big area in a short period while a course is building that it is unlikely that the fullest possible potential has been exploited. There will always be scope for refinement, for additional feature, for modification to meet minor situations that arise in play which it was neither practical nor perhaps possible to foresee initially. The Sixties saw most old cupboards cleared out because the golf course is an organic thing in every sense and the greatest courses of today are not those which have stood still over the years. They have grown, developed and matured with the help, in spite of what people say, of a committee. To admit this is not to belittle the original architect. Unless the framework is right, it is unlikely that any amount of subsequent local surgery will ever make it so. A major operation will be necessary. The duty of the Green Committee is to listen, to assess, sift, relate, and to discuss before investigating general opinion on modification. If the golf course architect can be brought into the discussion so much the better. It should, in fact, be routine after two years' play and it would be a stiff-necked man who claimed that his *a priori* judgements were better than those made on them *a posteriori*.

The worst error the Green Convener can make is to 'go it alone'. The mere fact that some feature is controversial and creating thoughts of change, indicates that it will have strong support in some quarters. If there was one good reason for putting a bunker in one place originally, there must be two to move it elsewhere.

Lastly comes the need to work out the logistics. A change which puts a hole out of action for a whole summer had better be good. The Green Committee, like the original construction, is likely to find itself reliant on weather. Perhaps even more so because what was once ploughed land is now fine turf and in play. An alteration which comes to a halt and hangs about unfinished while weeds grow may be doomed before it gets finished. We will consider later how best to prepare for modest changes and even big ones, but before that stage is reached, we will look in more detail at the fundamentals on which every golf course is planned, every hole designed, and some, subsequently, altered.

3 Planning

'A hole should always give one the
impression that it owes its existence to
its own intrinsic merits, to its
individuality and character, and not, as
too often happens, to the fact that it had
to be there because, forsooth, there was
no other place to put it.'

Garden G. Smith, *The World of Golf* (1898)

3.1 THE SITE

The site largely determines the character, quality and cost of the golf course; it can be ruined by inexperienced planning, design, or construction. Area is fundamental. Below 100 acres, length, interest, variety and safety tend to fall below desirable standards. Greater acreage gives scope for better planning, landscaping, separating holes, avoiding wet, steep or barren ground and for providing practice areas or a short relief course. Area is equally the determining factor in the benefits which additional land can bring to an existing course.

Gentle undulations with trees, features, and a light soil are preferable to sites dead flat, hilly or on heavy clay. The relief of monotonous ground is expensive if it is to be effective. Cheap fill may be available for moundwork but topsoil must still be stripped and replaced, drainage may need extra attention, and damage of heavy traffic, restored. Half the cost of a golf course built to a modern specification on a stiff clay may be attributed to improving porosity and drainage. If this is not done, future upkeep will be difficult and sometimes the course will be out of play. On public courses, that means loss of revenue; on private courses, discontented members.

The traditional home of golf on seaside links remains the model and some aspect of that type of land is generally echoed in a good inland course made at reasonable cost. But most new schemes will start from other considerations – land availability, development plan, location, access. Where there is any choice, the following eight 'S' factors should be compared – The Golf Development Council will help at this stage at negligible cost to the promoter.

Size

From 100 to 150 acres. On average ground, 120 acres will do very well. But a shorter course on less can still attract golfers.

Shape

Most arable farms have arrived at workable boundaries adaptable to golf course layout. Avoid necks or salients less than 400 feet wide. Prefer a single unit to one divided by roads.

Slopes

Steep uphill holes are never popular unless the ascent is short. Gentle undulations on a broad scale should predominate.

Soil

A spade's depth of medium or light loam with reasonably porous subsoil eliminates expensive importations, though sand and peat are generally used in a special mix on putting greens and tees. Sandy soils are preferable but fine, silty sands can cause trouble. Natural drainage is to be prized.

Land which has been down to grass for several years will be more amenable if disturbance is minimized. It works down to playable fairways in a season provided it is not rutted or heavily poached by cattle and is not churned up by contractor's plant during construction. But ask why it has not been turned over. Be suspicious of woodland areas.

Safety

Roads or houses on boundaries require wide safety margins and reduce effective acreage but form a protective barrier. The value of new plots will be much enhanced by the golf course. Footpaths through the site can also lead to danger unless avoidance or diversion is possible. Areas of common land introduce special problems, especially where there are commoners' rights.

Streams

Water can generally be worked into the layout to good effect. Streams can be widened or dammed to form pools and possibly provide or augment water supply. Flooding should be exceptional. Established lakes or ponds are valuable especially if the margins are approachable and not reedy.

Services

Water (1000 gallons per hour upwards). Electricity (preferably 3-phase if pumping has to be done). Connection to main sewer or private plant. Check underground pipelines, gas mains and wayleaves.

Storage

Existing buildings may be suitable for implement and compost sheds or for conversion to staff cottages. They are seldom suitable for clubhouses.

Given our site, we can now move on to arranging the layout within it.

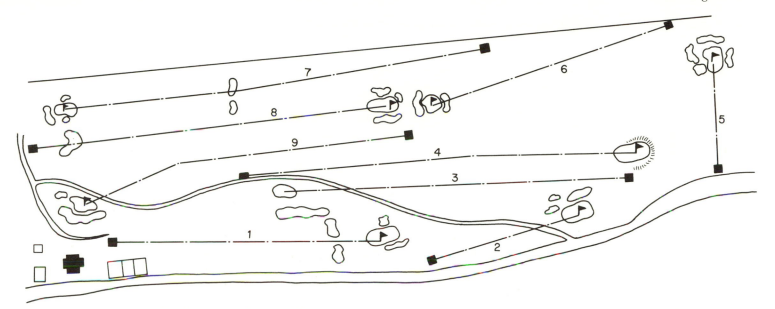

Fig. 3.1   An early French layout (at Tours), 1911. There appears to be congestion, and even danger, at 3, 4 and 9, but the plan is probably not to scale and there may only have been 20–30 members at the start. Bunkering is not all timeless, but no. 9 is a climax. Nine holes of average length inevitably lead to parallel holes on this type of site.

3.2   LAYOUT

James II was sent to Scotland, while still Duke of York. He played golf a good deal on the links at Leith in intervals between torturing Covenanters. These occupations – golf and torture – have been closely linked in the minds of the public ever since and there is an important sense in which the golf course architect must work within this contradiction. He must tease rather than bludgeon and never exhaust the victim physically. Therefore, abstract virtues like variety, balance, scale and beauty, influence purely practical aspects of planning and design. A 6000 yard course on a flat, featureless site, could be vastly more tiring than 7000 yards in wooded, gently rolling country. The formula eventually successful derives as much from landscape, player psychology and aesthetic considerations as from the golfing merits of 18 holes. The first true championship course was, in fact, on the links at Leith. At full stretch, it measured nine miles. Play, however, was provided with extra incentive by proceeding from one pub to another. It is no coincidence that a view of the Clubhouse beyond the 18th green is still a help to golfers tending to flag after 17 holes. On the other hand, Mr Chi Chi Rodriguez is said to have designed a course in his native Puerto Rico which consists of nineteen holes. His theory is that the first hole should never count.

Almost by accident, it has turned out that 18 holes is about right both in time and effort, and their pattern will produce or qualify the tensions, excitements and reliefs which inspire the golfer to play his best and leave him always hopeful of achieving more next time.

A second figure of note was the professional golfer, Tom Dunn, who whenever invited to give his opinion of a prospective golf course site, would always say 'God obviously intended this for a golf course'. But times have changed and Divine intentions can no longer be easily inferred. Factors like proximity to a million or more population, a motorway, planning permission for a thousand houses, the desire to outshine others, may well override (by justifying greater investment) factors like rock, bog, hills, or toxicity of the soil which would otherwise condemn the site absolutely. This equally applies to all reclamation jobs in Britain, if we run out of normal land.

The initial feasibility study by the golf architect today may, therefore, be as much an exercise in costing and mathematical assessment of possible routes for the 18 holes as an appreciation of merit. The range of his experience becomes daily more significant, for on basically unsuitable sites inexperience in architect or contractor can lead to extravagant errors. The final budget trimming process above all needs a mature hand. This is where the golf architect of experience will prune the specification to the bone and still produce an acceptable result.

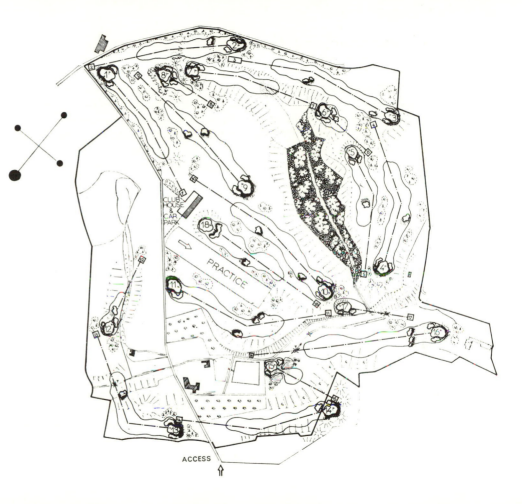

Fig. 3.2 Contour problems spread this layout over an area wider than normal but basic requirements are still provided: 1st and 10th tees close together for control, 18th green just below the clubhouse veranda, and practice areas close at hand. Total length could be varied from 5500 to 6700 yards. Five short holes are one more than average but a good short hole is generally preferable to a bad par 4. Dusseldorf Golf Club.

But historical influences still guide modern golf course developments in layout. The earliest players could only find playable grass on links land, dwarfed by drought and salt winds. Links land by its nature is a thin coastal strip and the earliest courses generally went out from the starting point for the first nine holes and came back to it with the second nine (e.g. St Andrews, Burnham and Berrow, Prestatyn). Later, the same pattern occurred with a Clubhouse more centrally situated (e.g. Western Gailes) and when the game moved inland, the convenience of a second starting point (preferably at no. 10 tee) on compact rather than linear sites, became virtually obligatory. Most of the new inland courses were of compact arrangement not only because that uses least land but also because golf adapts very well to the average-shaped farm of, say, 120 acres.

Entirely different considerations apply in any golf development involving housing. Plots with direct access to the course are more desirable than those in the second rank. Therefore, the length of the boundary of the golf course plays a vital role in profitability.

A compact layout on 144 acres could occupy a square with sides about half a mile long, thus producing two miles of marginal development. A linear layout of 7000 yards with nine holes out and nine back alongside, occupies a rectangle of, say, two miles long with potential marginal development of four miles. If the same length of linear layout is split into a single loop, one hole wide, the marginal development goes up to eight miles.

The ideal compromise for these purposes would, therefore, seem to be a two loop linear layout, that is to say, a figure 8 with a practice ground and the Clubhouse at the centre.

Where 27 or 36 holes are to be planned, identical considerations apply, although the increased congestion at the centre obviously pushes marginal development further out.

The ideal pattern, whatever other activities are intended, will not emerge until after several studies of land form, soil and drainage – with comparisons of possible alternatives. It must then not only produce a good golf course but also solve the relationship of the diverse elements to overall expenditure, and to each other.

Where residential development is of secondary importance, the compact – probably rectangular – layout, using minimum land, is likely to be the preferred answer. In extensive developments, the course will expand to match but the ultimate ideal will compromise with other factors. For example,

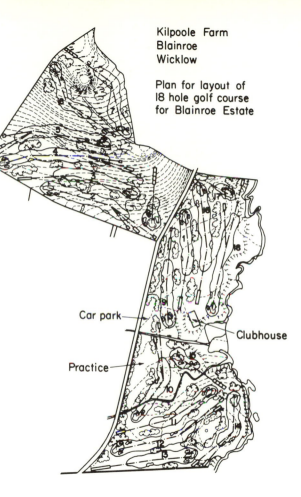

Kilpoole Farm
Blainroe
Wicklow

Plan for layout of
18 hole golf course
for Blainroe Estate

Car park

Clubhouse

Practice

Fig. 3.3   A new layout on cliff tops south of Wicklow (Kilpoole Farm, Blainroe).
The parallel series 2–6 is by no means ideal but the best solution to climbing
gently to the 6th green. Tree planting will eventually relieve any sense of tedium
but with spectacular marine and inland views must not be too dense.

the plots in the second line will be more valuable if they have at least a view of the golf course. Thus, the layout will tend to follow valleys while houses occupy the neighbouring slopes arranged wherever possible to look over those lower down.

Following valleys has a considerable effect on construction costs. More topsoil and less woodland, stone or rock may be met though surface drainage problems might arise. In a big development, the plots will absorb more constructional costs and the total plan may thus take higher priority than the golf course. In all the compromises, the golf architect must remain immovable against suggestions which he knows will not finally be acceptable to the golfer. The success of the golf course is the success of the project.

The type of Club to be formed will influence the type of course required. When all the basic golfing requirements have been met, there remains a certain margin within which specifications may differ according to eventual use as a private, proprietary, resort, hotel, sports centre, second home, or municipal development. Many developers will wish to have the type of golf course most likely to attract publicity and, therefore, think in terms of a 'championship' or 'international standard' golf course.

In Britain a 'championship' course is one where the Open Championship is played but the term has crept into wider use and is applied to courses with somewhere around 7000 yards total length. This length is quite unsuitable for most golfers for whom 6300 is already a good test. The back tees will, therefore, seldom be used. But a championship course involves many features beyond length – good viewing facilities, space for crowd movement, tentage and car-parking; easy access by road; and plenty of hotel accommodation. The need for stewarding also presupposes a large number of willing local amateur golfers prepared to steward crowds for a few days. They may be less willing to do this for what they see as a purely commercial venture than they are for the normal sponsored event.

A professional tournament can be arranged wherever enough money is provided. One Spanish resort golf course staged the Spanish Open Championship for five years in succession by suitable financial guarantees. However, the refusal of permission for a casino upset all calculations and these five years were wasted. A golf course needs local support as well as championships.

Similar considerations affected the holding of what was then the Canada Cup in Paris at St Nom La Bretèche, only a couple of years after opening. This development consisted of two compact 18 hole courses of three loops with one group of island housing but otherwise all marginal plots surrounding the valley. The developers reckoned that the holding of this international competition advanced sales by at least two years. But so far as the golf course is concerned it is generally better to wait an extra year rather than open before the turf is strong.

The desire for the ultimate in length and prestige can be satisfied on big sites but must be restrained elsewhere. There is no swifter road to failure than putting a quart-sized golf course into a pint-sized acreage.

3.3   GUIDELINES

Dr Mackenzie's thirteen points which were summarized earlier included two on future maintenance. We could, however, categorize these under 'Utility' if we analyse the thought which must precede building a golf course, a hole, or even one bunker. Under five headings, we will re-arrange the important considerations that have so far been introduced. The first three are strategy, variety and beauty.

Strategy

Siting of hazards positive: to encourage *placing* shots to secure subsequent advantage; not to aid judgement of line or distance; not simply to punish the wild shot.
- Siting, slope, shape, orientation and bunkering of green to influence play from tee onwards.
- Use of irregular and oblique slopes, especially on approaches.
- Use of deceptive distances and dead ground.
- Use of contour to obscure green or approach from certain angles.
- Wholly blind shots and concealed hazards to be exceptional or avoided. Bottom of flag-stick visible at short holes; flag and something of green at others.
- Alternative tees to suit weather conditions and standards of play.

Variety

In length, direction and character of consecutive holes and shots.
- All types of shot to be demanded, none excessively.
- In formation of greens and green surfaces: in fairway slopes and outlines; in type, form, siting and alignment of hazards.
- In distribution and length of short holes and par 5s.
- In alternative tees to vary line.

Beauty

Artificial work indiscernible from natural formation: balance and formality avoided.
- Carefully planned site clearance and tree felling.
- Judicious planting of trees and shrubs to enhance the site and conceal external distractions.
- Use of planting, water, sand.
- Use of vistas, background, perspective, surprise, climax.
The last two headings are economy and utility.

Economy

Site to dictate broad outlines of plan: maximum use of natural feature. Landscape effects also derived from site. Earth movement planned for dual purpose when possible (i.e. cut to form one feature provides fill to form another).
- Minimum bunkers for control of play.
- Precise seed and fertiliser rates. Permeability tests to determine exact proportions of soil/sand/peat for green mix.
- Husbandry of water resources.

Utility

(a) In play
- Course to suit site and type of use; not to be tiring: direct uphill slopes avoided.
- Two or more starting points.
- Short walks from greens to following tees preferably forward.
- Westward holes avoided in second half.
- No 'impossible' lies in bunkers or slopes on greens.
- Greens to be capable of receiving approach shot planned.
- Adequate safety margin.
- Provision for crowd control.

(b) In maintenance
- Minimum hand labour needed.
- Adequate teeing-grounds and alternative tees, winter and summer.
- Adequate green area and space for changing holes.
- 'Frost' greens.
- Practice ground/practice bunkers.
- Practice putting green.
- Turf nursery.
- Adequate drainage and top soil (= specialist advice).
- Adequate water system (greens, tees, and where necessary, fairways.)

The first three points under economy are chiefly concerned with layout. A carefully prepared plan can save hundreds of pounds without in any way detracting from the ultimate merits of the result. This applies as much to choice of the position for tees or bunkers as to the selection of green sites. Given a good site, the really successful plan produces good golf with simplicity and the minimum of soil shifting. Today more than ever, only those bunkers necessary to govern play and give interest are made. Apart from the money they cost to construct, there comes afterwards the steady expense of raking, weeding, trimming the faces, and providing sand. This is so much money wasted unless the bunker is doing its job.

Considerations of Utility have been divided into those concerning play and those concerning maintenance. The first group represents to some extent the pressure exerted on design by the problem of handling large numbers of players with safety and despatch. This is abundantly clear in the design of public and municipal courses which have become a specialized study in their own right. One American operator insists that the longer a public course, the more players can be squeezed on to it. It seems to me more important to get them round it and off it, just as many clubs put tees forward in winter.

However, it must be admitted that the cost of making a long course is not significantly greater than making a short one of similar standing; and that writers have been grumbling for 80 years about courses getting longer with no apparent effect. Now we are promised more yards from a golf ball with a different arrangement of dimples and some subtle changes in dimple design.

The total effect of all these economic and utilitarian considerations is to discipline the designer and define the field within which he must achieve his perfection. The ideal course today is only to be completed after long and arduous preliminaries, but, on that score alone, it is the more precious and worthwhile.

The second group of notions under utility concerns the usefulness of the course in upkeep. Constructional work produces gradients that tractor and gangs or ride-on mowers can cover in at least one direction. Bunker shapes, tee banks, featuring-all contour changes are subject to the same considerations. The problems of wear can be overcome; the course will never be out of play; the greenkeeper's life, relatively, will be a happy one.

3.4   REHEARSAL

At the risk of seeming repetitive we can now put history and current practice together to summarize the basis of a full-scale layout again before we conclude with shorter alternatives.

Whatever type of golf club is to be formed, the course must make full use of the land while providing for foreseeable contingencies of local development. The plan should secure the utmost practical advantage while using every element of the site likely to give pleasure and interest in play. It will achieve effect with economy, compromise wisely and preserve landscape.

The total length of eighteen holes will normally exceed 6000 yards, but this is not obligatory. Relatively few golfers benefit from 7000 yards, but it has a certain prestige value amongst the uninitiated and for courses associated with hotels or residential development. A good standard length is still about 6350 yards or in the 6201 to 6400 yards range (5670 to 5852 metres). But much more length is needed at considerable altitude where the air is thin and the ball flies further.

The mainstay of most clubs is the middle handicap golfer for whom forward tees, except in competitions, are desirable. Public courses will often be shorter still, owing to the high proportion of beginners and the need to speed play.

An average course will comprise:

Four or five holes, 130–200 yards, par 3, 120–180 metres.
Nine or ten holes, 350–470 yards, par 4, 320–430 metres.
Three or four holes, 480–550 yards, par 5, 440–500 metres.

Holes between 230 and 320 yards, 210 and 295 metres, are best avoided, though one or two are often inevitable in restricted areas, and, if provocatively designed, may achieve distinction.

Long par 5 holes, need feature and careful treatment to avoid monotony. The ideal plan will contrive a range of holes and use of ground to test every club in the bag. The first hole will be a straightforward par 4, or a shortish par 5. The remainder will vary in length, character and direction, with short 3s and long 5s well distributed, preferably allotted equally between the two halves and never consecutive, although in championship layouts a run of par 5s in the last few holes will stiffen the end of the round. There should be as few closely parallel holes as possible avoiding an east to west direction later in the round. Lines of play will never produce mutual interference. Approach to higher ground should be oblique. The first and 10th tees (also, if possible, others) and the 9th and 18th greens should be in front of or near the clubhouse with practice ground close at hand. A practice putting green should be near the 1st tee.

Fig. 3.4   The 16th green fits snugly into the clubhouse surrounds at Royal Waterloo, Brussels. The 9th and 18th do the same at the front of the building towards the left of the picture.

An experienced golf course architect will incorporate as many natural tee and green sites, approaches, features, and interesting contours as overriding requirements of the plan permit, effecting great economies in this way. He is generally, indeed, the only person able to handle the complicated relationship between site characteristics, method, cost of construction, cash flow, upkeep, the game and, eventually, the psychological reaction of players.

Modifications of natural land-forms and the construction of additional featuring will complete or form greens, bunkers and approaches or, more rarely, areas of fairway. New work must merge imperceptibly with ground not disturbed and match the character of the site. All slopes should be unobjectionable in play and inexpensive in upkeep. The finest work will be as indistinguishable from natural contours as it is distinctively bold, imaginative and exciting.

3.5   SHORT ALTERNATIVES

Existing golf courses often wish they could expand. Nine hole courses particularly wish to go to 18. Recognizing that desire, it is often a difficult task to advise a hopeful Green Committee that an additional area will only get them up to 5400 yards where twice round their present nine holes is 6400. But on the whole, 18 holes below normal standard length will always be preferable to nine and will certainly permit the club to move forward in membership and usefulness.

18 hole courses may also experience the same need to expand. Ideally, another full-scale 9 holes bring immense relief to congestion and the problem of separating beginners from others more experienced, particularly at public courses. In Dublin when the City turned down the Irish Golf Union's suggestion for Phoenix Park, Christopher Gaisford St Lawrence planned 18 holes pitch and putt, 18 holes par 3 and 27 holes full scale, later extended to 36, in the grounds of Howth Castle. He built a clubhouse, with adjoining hotel and facilities for receptions, over-looking Dublin Bay on one side and Portmarnock Bay and the Eye of Ireland on the other. Phasing the construction work, he completed the golf elements with estate labour resources. This was the first public course in Ireland and it has never looked back. This form also produces interesting possibilities of combination: A + B, A + C, B + C and, of course, the other way round and even

more with D. But where a full scale layout is not possible, small marginal areas can sometimes be found which will help a junior section, the professional's tuition, and indeed the member pressed for time on the way to the office, from the office, or between the two.

The possibility of reducing the length of a 9 hole course by increasing the number of par 3 holes leads eventually to the par 3 course, in principle a layout of holes on a full scale but all between 100 and 200 yards or 90 and 180 metres, approximately. In practice longer holes are sometimes included where space permits but their value and usefulness are open to question.

This form of layout is very flexible and no rigid standards are laid down though the basic considerations of interest and informality in design and safety and variety in layout are vital. It is also adaptable to terrain where par 4 holes would not be feasible owing to rugged contour. On an 18 hole course, the short holes frequently occur at points where water, valleys, quarries or similar obstacles would otherwise make the connection of the holes on either side very difficult. A par 3 hole with virtually no fairway surmounts the obstacles and benefits from the drama which they impart. A series of par 3 holes can tolerate a series of obstacles where longer holes would be no more than eccentric. This form of layout may therefore be appropriate to a piece of land which does not recommend itself for normal recreations, though too many steep climbs will be no more popular than they are on other courses and routine maintenance operations must not be unduly complicated.

Broadly speaking, the par 3 course can help to bridge the gap between the number of golfers and of holes to accommodate them, because its smaller area and costs are more easily provided. It is nevertheless an attempt to reproduce most of the problems and conditions of normal golf and the care devoted to its design, construction, and maintenance should not be scaled down in proportion to the acreage.

The space should be adequate to provide safety margins even better than might be acceptable on the full-scale course and play should be directed away from boundaries. Thus for nine par 3 holes some fifteen acres should be provided with proportionately more if one or two longer holes are included or if some of the land cannot be employed in the layout.

Wear on the turf will be intense so it is normal to provide rubber or nylon matting for tees, while greens should not be smaller than 250–350 yd² (210–290m²). Green design and bunkers must be carefully related to golfing needs if the total effect is to be rewarding for the player.

A favourable situation for a par 3 course is in conjunction with a driving range. It can then expand the limitations of that field of operation and complement the playing experience which can be gained. Regular attendance at a driving range presupposes a certain interest in the game and therefore the nearer any additional facilities approach normal golf, the greater the encouragement to progress. Since professional instructors are often in attendance the elements of golfing etiquette are also likely to be acquired at the same time.

The final recourse, and by no means an unattractive one, is the 'Pitch and Putt' course, the most adaptable of all forms of small-scale golf. It has several practical advantages. Holes may range from 30 yards to 90 yards (25 to 80 metres) though 70 yards (65 metres) is generally a useful maximum. Since novices with no judgement of distance or direction can be expected, the safety factor must be carefully studied both internally and externally. Holes closely parallel to a boundary or playing towards one will be avoided, with hole lengths kept down on small sites. Eight acres, or rather more than 3 hectares, is just enough for eighteen holes of varied length. On a lesser acreage, holes must be shorter and planned so as to minimize danger.

Planting and landscaping can receive generous treatment on this relatively small area to increase attractiveness. Hazards can be included for interest but only where the direction of play will be towards a safe area.

Greens will not be much bigger than 150 to 250 yd² (125 to 210m²) and tee-mats will be obligatory. Green size can be near the minimum if the course will be closed in winter but the standard of preparation and design should otherwise be equivalent to that for a full-size course if proper golfing conditions and problems are to be presented. Heavy use is synonymous with adequate green area to change hole positions.

Only two clubs, a lofted iron and a putter, are required. This simplifies equipping players and speeds play.

If all else fails, there are three hole layouts with three sets of tees at each hole. After that, as always, back to the practice ground.

4 Design

'Any man who dreams that the golf
course he has laid out will meet with
universal approval is doomed to
disappointment.'

Garden G. Smith, *The World of Golf* (1898)

4.1 TEES

(a) General location

The earliest rules of golf stipulated that the ball must be teed within a certain number of club lengths of the previous hole.

Willie Park in 1896 said 'tees should be placed on level parts of the course if possible with a slight slope upward in the direction to be played'. Since in the same article he said 'that greens should only be constructed artificially as a last resource', we may assume that there were still no artificially constructed tees.

The first mention of providing a teeing area by specific turfing appears two years later. We have been burdened with them ever since.

The concentration of all players each day into a small strip of perhaps, less than 15 square yards to start the play of each hole is already a problem. When, in addition to trampling the area with studded shoes, they beat it with wooden or iron clubs and remove slices from its surface, there is clearly need for thoughtful design and continuing maintenance. The factors most likely to be determinant are location and area.

Location will limit area locally but must not reduce the total provided at each hole. It will also affect the form, gradient and surroundings of each tee.

The successful tee will be near enough to the preceding green, clear of overhanging trees, will allow a view of the fairway at the end of the drive, will fit into the landscape discreetly and not deceive the player by false orientation or levels. It will provide a test of skill relative to the players' ability and the season. Finally, although its situation may be exciting and the view impressive, the final test of a good tee is that it should otherwise be totally unremarkable in all respects save for its impeccable surface.

One authority has suggested that wherever possible a tee should be no further from the previous green than 60 yards or 55 metres. This is a good rule. Long walks from greens to tees intrude on the even progress of the round, cause mild irritation (especially if they involve walking back over ground which will be covered in the play of the hole) and, generally, are the first and most obvious target for criticism. No amount of academic explanation – benefits to total length, need for a par 5, a better length par 4, provision of a par 3 requiring a wooden club – will ever properly compensate for the element of tedium introduced. This restriction applies still more forcibly to alterations to existing holes or rearrangements of sequence to provide some imagined benefit. Such changes especially must be free of this taint if they are to succeed and survive.

Where the need for above average distance between holes can be clearly demonstrated by topographical feature, then the golf course architect or the green convener may feel more secure. If nobody can make any practical suggestion for bringing two holes closer together, then the inevitable separation will settle down with only the occasional distant rumble of complaint.

But this licence will apply mostly to mountainous and hilly sites or to those broken by rock, water or other accidents of terrain which a par 3 hole cannot bridge. It is not to be relied on in less severe situations, nor repeated too often within 18 holes whatever its inevitability.

The factors determining the proximity of the tee to the preceding green are normally as follows:

1. *Distance* A reasonable distance is desirable to avoid mutual disturbance by sight or sound between adjacent tees and greens and moreover disturbance by player circulation where, as is

sometimes necessary, the layout contains loops of holes which are intertwined and not distinct with each nine hole loop complete within itself.

2.   *Visibility*   The drop of the tee shot should preferably be seen from the tee. Semi-blindness (e.g. a brow at 100 yards from the tee) is not acceptable because of the danger and boredom it produces.

3.   *Elevation*   The second desideratum is more likely to be achieved from a situation on an eminence than at the foot of an uphill slope, or at the worst, in a hollow. In dune country, what has come to be known as a 'pulpit' tee is not unusual though the classical amateur will object that greatest skill is involved in moving the ball the right distance from a tee to a green both at sea level. This is true. But it throws us back to the basic choice between what type of golf course we want. A tee which is elevated, affording a handsome view of the Channel or Mediterranean, large enough to take the wear, inspiring confidence and pleasure in most players and presenting the hole almost as a broad plan instead of a thin elevation, may finally cause the rout of the classical few by the romantic many. And why not? The third and the old fifteenth tees at Goodwood take advantage of the strong contours of the South Downs. Coming back to Goodwood forty years after playing round the course with my father in 1935, both were still clear in my memory, though less spectacular holes had faded.

(b) In trees
Where the tee is sited among trees several additional requirements must be observed respectfully. It is not uncommon moreover that holes are lengthened by putting tees back into trees where the work involved was not considered cost-effective in earlier days. Both in hot climates and those more temperate, problems of upkeep and play will arise unless a well-rounded operation is mounted.

Firstly, roots must be properly extracted to avoid future subsidence and before that operation is completed the clearing made should be checked for:

1. *Width* Does it fan out quickly enough to avoid a rebound likely to return on the striker? Are the trees so close to the sides of teeing area that players will instinctively tee up down the centre of the tee, wasting potential use of the two sides? This factor also applies where the clearing out to the fairway is too narrow so that fear of hitting the sides makes the centre of the tee the logical starting point.

2. *Overhang* Do tree tops overhang the teeing area? Drip and shade will surely kill the grass. Will tree tops overhang in the future? Better take out the tree likely to offend at once while the machinery and muddle are going on.

3. *Air* Can air circulate to dry out the tee surface – a pocket of still air will not encourage healthy growth.

4. *Frost* Has thought been given to sunshine in winter – a permafrost tee will be of no benefit.

5. *Soil* Has soil for the surface been imported – trees are often planted on unproductive, infertile, or mechanically undesirable soils.

6. *Types* Are the trees of types like chestnuts and sycamores which will deposit a wet blanket on the grass in the autumn and effectively kill any grass that has managed to survive the summer?

7. *Roots* Will marginal trees be far enough away for roots not to compete with the grass or even to invade the surface? In warmer climates eucalyptus and wattle trees positively pump out all available moisture for their own benefit.

8. *Grass species* From time to time one sees advertised 'woodland' mixtures of grass seed. These

may like shade but they will not like close mowing and offer no alternative to the normal practice of providing light, air and water in ordinary quantities and by ordinary means.

If we can derive any general code from these warnings, it could be summed up by suggesting that practical requirements will probably require the removal of about twice as many trees as expected. Moreover, unless this is done, it is unlikely that the aesthetically elegant margins of clearing which will finally seal its success, will ever be achieved.

(c) On slopes

A situation at the foot of rising ground has to be treated carefully (see also *Gradient* below) but provided there is even a brief moment of descent at the front of the tee before the rise begins it can be made acceptable. Clearly the further back the tee can be made from the rise the better the effect, but if a tee is all made on the slope it is surprising how quickly the back of a lengthened formation begins to get too high and disagreeable. The need to make a tee in this position may, however, be due to failure at the planning stage, especially if a less frontal attack on the rise could be contrived. If it cannot, it is better, where possible to retire to a down-slope further back.

Tees to be built on slopes need particular forethought in deciding the most suitable formation. The drawback of excessive build-up applies equally to tees built on strong forward slopes. The difficulty arises when the flat, top surface cannot be connected to a slope falling away from it by any reasonable gradient. An unlikely section of a pyramid is thus left obstructing the landscape. The solutions found for this problem are three-fold:

1.   In mountain courses (Mont-Agel, the Monte Carlo Golf Club course, has several examples and there are others at Valcros near Hyères at the other end of the Côte d'Azur) the effort of

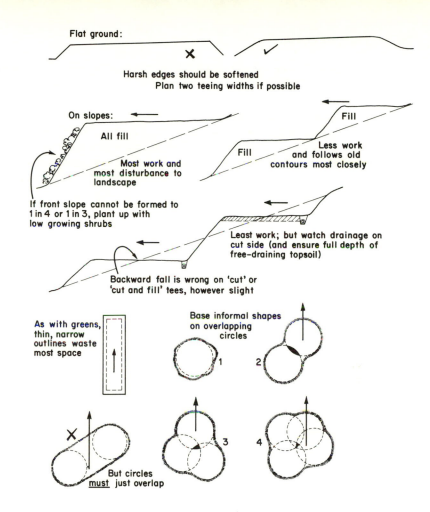

Flat ground:

Harsh edges should be softened
Plan two teeing widths if possible

On slopes:

All fill

Fill

Fill

Most work and
most disturbance to
landscape

Less work
and follows old
contours most closely

If front slope cannot be formed to
1 in 4 or 1 in 3, plant up with
low growing shrubs

Least work; but watch drainage on
cut side (and ensure full depth of
free-draining topsoil)

Backward fall is wrong on 'cut' or
'cut and fill' tees, however slight

As with greens,
thin, narrow
outlines waste
most space

Base informal shapes
on overlapping
circles

1

2

3

4

But circles
must just overlap

Fig. 4.1   Tees.

incorporation in the landscape is frankly abandoned and a stone wall substituted.

The wall will usually be built in local stone and must provide for drainage in the form of weep holes if the stones are laid with mortar. A wooden rail should be installed on the high side but, obviously, not at the front. Fortunately, no accidents due to players falling from the front of a high tee are known, but in extreme situations some form of safety ledge at a lower level could also be provided. Even if players are restricted to teeing well back from the front edge, ground staff with motor mowers may be at risk, especially in confined spaces. The stone wall may also be necessary to level up a path alongside a tee built on sharp slopes and one wall can sometimes be contrived to serve both purposes.

2.   In sandy country, old railway sleepers have been used to perform the same function to restrict the outward extent of tee banks and they are occasionally seen inland. Their effect is acceptable on links of a certain age where traditional appearances have persisted and they are still more frequently used simply as steps down from high tees. Unless well stabilized by iron supports (and this is difficult to achieve without visual objections) they should not be used beyond their strict engineering limits. In fact in all matters where support, stress and stability factors occur, it would be wise to take advice from a member with an engineering background if a permanent solution is to be found.

3.   Many of the problems arising from tee positions on slopes will be much reduced if a random or at least a rounded outline is adopted. Indeed where the bank already needs support by wall or piling, a less rigid form will be more agreeable to the eye. The informal shape, however, should still be related in some sense to the line of play or at least not be misleading.

Where the line of play is close to being at right angles to a sharp gradient, a tee narrow from front to back and long from side to side will require less material and be less obvious in appearance.

Where this form is selected, careful attention should be paid to access which must be provided at least at either end and preferably also at intervals along the breadth from behind. If traffic is obliged to use the tee itself to reach the section in use then the passage of many feet will give no respite to areas which need rest. A tee made on these lines should in any case exceed the average standards of area.

(d) Distribution

The problems just discussed will be exaggerated if the legitimate goal of single large teeing areas for easier maintenance and maximum distribution of wear, is applied perversely to the wrong situation – that is to say in broken, sharply undulating ground. In sand dunes, the formation of one large tee should only be attempted if it is certain that the landscape will not be disturbed. Dispersal of the teeing areas in positions involving only local disturbance will preserve more of the natural flora, cost less, and vary the traffic pattern to advantage. Other factors important in play may also be better served, either alone or in combination – different angles of attack to bunkering, different effects of slope in fairways, or protection from wind when estimating drift. It is by no means certain that the large single tee is appropriate where the contours of the site are severe. A very flexible approach to the provision of adequate teeing areas must be maintained and the interests of easy maintenance may have to be sacrificed here and there, to preserve more of the intrinsic quality of the golf and the landscape.

Where 7000 yards (6400 metres) is provided off single long tees there is anything from 500 to 800 yards (455 to 730 metres) between the back markers and those from which the typical client is not overtaxed. Tees which were 60 yards or 55 metres long would provide a variety of length from 6000 to 7000 yards, but the head greenkeeper will require a detailed chart and computer programme to deliver 6500 yards while at the same time fully employing the back 30 yards of each tee. The lesson is that long tees may be wasteful while long, thin tees will be even more so.

From the Pyrenees southward, play is less intense except close to big cities like Barcelona where El Prat and San Cugat take a tremendous hammering but grass growth is nearly continuous so less wear problems arise. But the risks should be borne in mind if a pattern of this sort is translated to the west of Scotland. Where winter rainfall is significant, 'Championship' length may be better achieved by concentrating the bulk of the teeing space at rational distances and confining the champions to individual tees appropriately remote.

Lastly, at holes where the descent in front of the tee is abrupt, the long single tee will not be appropriate because the front edge will hide the fairway when viewed from the back. In this situation, tees must either be stepped down as required or staggered in echelon. This factor operates surprisingly often, even on gently undulating ground, and the back section or sections of a long tee will very often be better elevated above the rest.

Where tees are separated, the possibility of different lines of attack on the hole is opened up and variety in this respect is surprisingly refreshing quite apart from the advantages to distributing wear. We saw earlier that H.S. Colt pointed this out. Such advantages are particularly marked where two tees can be made to either side of the preceeding green so that, in combination with hole placement, one side of the green and its surrounds can be rested.

This endeavour is particularly valuable on 9 hole courses so that different tees can be used in the homeward half, more especially as traffic on a nine hole course is still more concentrated. In practice the alternative tees are frequently shorter than those built for maximum length so that total length is reduced by this device. Nevertheless the reduction will be of greater benefit in the long term than extra yards.

(e) Area
Factors of situation previously discussed will modify the area of teeing space which will, or can be, provided. Further factors of soil, drainage, growth and play will decide how much of that area will restore itself after use and how quickly. With all these variables any standard set for total area must equally fluctuate and the figures suggested are only a guide for new construction. They should be varied as local requirements indicate or experience demands.

The rotation adopted for the use of grass tees in summer will be a matter for the head greenkeepers' discretion especially in relation to competition tees and their preservation for the more important fixtures. It will be a matter of fact whether extent and conditions are such that teeing areas, once used, are able to recover before their turn for use comes round again. Once their surface starts to resemble the goal mouths of the average football field, it is too late to avoid returfing or renovation. There are intermediate measures possible in spring and autumn to accelerate recovery with judicious use of compost, seed and fertilizer but all such operations rely on adequate reserves of teeing space elsewhere while they are going on.

On public courses, with day-long traffic in all weather, it is probable that no sufficient area could ever be provided economically or practically to provide grass tees throughout the year. In winter, therefore, with little or no growth, the use of winter tees will be obligatory, as it will be on private courses where soil and area factors are substandard.

From general considerations, it is suggested that initially the specification (which will normally be metric) for the tees on a new course should call for not less than 300–350 m² at par 4s and 5s and 400–450 m² at par 3 holes. Where tees are separated, the apportionment of 350 m² might be:

    100 m² Back
    200 m² Middle and forward
     50 m² Ladies
    (In yd², add about 20%.)

The relatively small ladies' teeing area is not due to male chauvinism but to the extreme care with which they treat any area dedicated to their use. And there are generally rather less of them. When joined the total area might be pruned, if all on one level, because the loss of employable space is reduced. Assuming the front and back 1 metre of a tee 10 m by 10 m are scarcely used, the gain by conjunction is 20% and this is considerable in relation to a limited total area.

Where a tee is built transversely to the line of play, e.g. 35 metres wide by 10 metres depth, the loss is exaggerated compared with a single tee made 10 metres wide by 35 metres long depth – 20% as against about 6%. Thus, even on a tight budget the lower standard should only be provided in favourable circumstances. The higher standard can be exceeded where it is thought that this provision will be of more advantage to the ultimate success of the layout than in other departments where economies can be made initially at least and further development undertaken over the first few years.

(f) Gradient
It is desirable that the upper surface of the tee should possess a subtle gradient scarcely, if at all, visible to the player but strong enough to promote some surface flow of water when there is heavy rain, melting snow, or indeed any need to evacuate excess water, even after irrigation. There is a tendency for areas intensively used to become not only compacted but also slightly hollowed compared with the rest of the tee surface and a gradient will avoid ponding. Greatest use will generally occur down the centre.

   As a general guide, tees at uphill holes should slope upwards from back to front and those at downhill holes, downwards. The gradient provided should be of the order of 1:100. This is virtually unnoticeable in practice but the improved surface drainage provided matches the requirements of the tee shot. Where a tee is built by cut and fill on a down slope to limit the build-up of the front, it is absolutely essential that the downward slope from the back be provided and possibly a catchwater drain round the cut section as well to stop surface flow from outside increasing the amount of water arriving on the tee.

   Tees on side slopes can be provided with a cross fall of a similar proportion and indeed it may be desirable to do so because the outer edge of a platform levelled out of a slope tends to look much higher than the inside edge if the formation is made to true levels. A cross fall will make the formation 'look' level and this is the final touchstone. The golfer will just as readily complain about the tee which is actually level but, due to its situation in strong contours, looks otherwise.

   The provision of a camber on tees on heavy soil to shed water where one long gradient is inappropriate is a delicate operation. It is probably too subtle for contract work where a full 18 holes are under construction with all the pressures on time and labour which programme, weather and potential profit produce. The greenkeeper constructing a single tee may consider it but in these days the preferred use of free draining soil mixtures on the surface should obviate the need for special cambering.

One word of warning is, however, relevant to tees constructed by machine, then cultivated by tractor and agricultural implements, and finally harrowed, fertilized, sown and harrowed again. If the operations are repeated often enough, the level surface will slowly disappear leaving a cambered formation (or even domed on small tees). The grade developed on the sides may have crept too far inwards seriously restricting future use and nullifying the saving of time and manpower. Some kind of final levelling operation before sowing must be undertaken and it is likely to be best achieved by level pegs, board and manual corrections. When soil is at the cultivated stage it is difficult to estimate by eye the precision of a running level.

(g) Plan

The rectangular shape with sides parallel to the line of play entered into the vocabulary at the end of the nineteenth century and it has stayed popular ever since. It can be carried out well or ill and the first thing to avoid is a sharp angled edge. The size of the original formation should be large enough to provide the desired area after all the edges have been fully rounded off.

If this action is taken and the external slopes are swept out and married carefully into the surroundings then the aesthetic objection to the 'mechanical' type of tee can be much reduced. On flat land, clearly, the less the build-up, the less obvious the formation. This style of tee is certainly needed on courses where maintenance will be limited and it may be necessary from time to time to mow out tees with a light tractor and gang-mowers; to avoid scalping, the tee's upper edges must have been softened almost to the point of disappearing.

In most situations, an ugly tee bank can be masked by suitable planting or allowed to grow wild. The plants selected should be slow growing and low in height, bushy, and undemanding; heather is

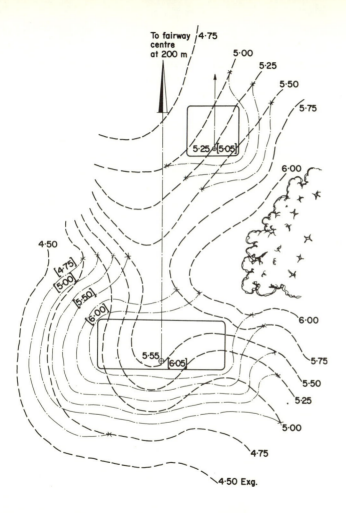

Fig. 4.2   Tee plan with existing and new contours. Contour interval: 0.25 m.

the obvious choice in an acid soil though some lime tolerant varieties might be tried elsewhere.

The degree of wildness allowed to develop where the other alternative is adopted will depend on local factors as well as personal taste. A lush growth of Yorkshire Fog or *Holcus mollis* is somehow inimical to good presentation whereas a bank of tufty *Fescue* is not.

The informal random-shaped tee is relatively rare on older courses although it has lately made a comeback under the influence of changed attitudes to landscape and a deeper search for perfection in golf-course shaping. It has the advantages described earlier in relating it to the landscape in difficult contours but it still seems necessary, if the golfer is not to be upset, to provide the sense of orientation given by the rectangular form. Perhaps that suggestion might be better put in a negative way. The random tee will not be successful if its general form directs or seems to direct the player on a line which is not ostensibly correct. Thus a perfectly circular tee, though hardly desirable aesthetically, would be acceptable in play since there would be no hint of orientation whatever. It is therefore suggested that the random tee will be best formed as a development of an implicit rectangle and that variations on its sides should average out in the best orientation.

However, the rounded formation is by no means excluded if the rules for the avoidance or concealment of edges and banks applicable to rectangular tees are equally applied to round ones. Indeed these rules are applicable to the raised edges of all grassland formations.

The design of the informally shaped tee will normally facilitate maintenance by ride-on mowers through the avoidance of square corners. By the same token their 'randomness' should not extend to the provision of thin wedges or sharp points difficult to bring into a mowing pattern and, abroad especially, into a watering pattern.

There is no reason why existing formal shapes should not in many instances be made informal simply by modifying the pattern of mowing where it is judged that this will facilitate maintenance and not much reduce the teeing area available.

Where rectangular tees are the rule, their alignment must be impeccable. Curious things can happen to the ball struck from a tee falsely oriented. There is an instinctive tendency for the arc of the swing of less experienced players to follow the line of the side of the tee even if the stance is taken up for another angle. The left-hander should also be remembered in this respect.

Players notice this fault less quickly than others more obvious but once it has been detected there will be no withstanding the tide of complaints. But detection will be slow where the tee edges are soft and not firmly lined up. As a temporary measure, adjustment of the mown outline may suffice.

There may be some doubt as to what is a true alignment of a tee. Taking a 120 yard, par 3 as an example, a rectangular tee with both sides aligned to the centre of the green would be perceptibly narrower at the front. A tee 30 yards by 10 yards wide at the back would be only some $7\frac{1}{2}$ yards wide at the front. There is no objection to this reduction in principle nor will it be very obvious in a tee of that length but as the flag position will vary by some five yards to each side of the centre line it seems preferable to establish a true rectangle based on the axis through the centres of the tee and the green. In practice, once the axis of the hole is established, the sides can be lined up by eye from the two back corners. A useful test to check alignment is to take up stance by reference only to the side of the tee and then look up to see if the shot would be directed to the green centre.

(h) Paths; steps

Owing to the disastrous effects on turf of golf shoes with soles isolated from the ground by a forest of metal studs, the wear round tees as well as on them, has increased to the point where eventually all areas of concentrated traffic must be given an artificial surface. This clearly applies particularly to tees. In the United States the tarmac paths made for buggies will already cope with this need. Courses on the Lancashire coast have mostly provided themselves with paths alongside tees and in the carry to fairways, surfaced with the red pit-mound ash and edged with tarred railway sleepers, the greenkeeper's perennial stand-by.

The cheapest local material whether it be stone, ash, hoggin, or indeed tarmac will probably be suitable. Gravels are perhaps to be treated with caution as they lead to scattered stones when the surface breaks down causing mowing problems. There are, however, some excellent binding products of crushed stone, quarry waste, and materials used for all-weather playing surfaces for other sports. These are probably to be preferred aesthetically to products derived from tar or bitumen once the club-house has been left behind. However the greenkeeper who resorts to the most durable surface in desperation (and this includes concrete slabs) should receive every sympathy especially where, as is probable, he is under pressure to concentrate on work more directly concerned with playing conditions.

The benefits of a made-up path alongside a tee will be nullified if the bank between path and tee is then destroyed by random scrambling from one level to the other. Thus, where there is a significant change of level between path and teeing area, the provision of steps is likely to be needed unless initial construction has been to a high standard especially in respect of easy gradients, the desirability of which constantly recurs in all aspects of golf course construction, and I am afraid, in this book, both on aesthetic and practical grounds.

It appears that any slope when walked on by many studded shoes starts to break up more quickly than flat ground. This is especially true where the slope is sideways to the line of progress and some degree of side-slip occurs. The progression from path to tee is likely to be at a right angle to the maximum angle of the slope but the nearer that slope approaches the horizontal the less the grass will suffer.

Thought could be given to the possibility (mentioned earlier) of leaving the grass to grow to its natural length. Unmown, it may survive longer since it is under less stress and any unkempt appearance, produced by traffic will to some extent be counteracted by the absence of fine cutting.

Where none of these measures produce the necessary diminution in wear then steps will be needed. Whether these be of brick, stone, concrete or wood is probably of less importance than the provision of enough points of access to ensure that the wear avoided on banks is not transferred to the upper surface of the tee itself.

Steps which merely concentrate traffic on to one part of the tee, from which players proceed to the day's markers, may cause more obvious problems. The ideal would be a made-up path parallel with the right side of the tee from which at any point one could step directly on to the tee itself.

Fig. 4.3 Substituting this low wall for the original grass bank kept trolleys off this tee at one of the Melbourne courses.

Trolleys would then be left where they should be – off one side of the tee – and progress would be rational and uncomplicated. The path should normally be on the right though the side chosen is virtually unconnected with right or left handedness. Access to the teeing position can just as readily be gained from the left of the tee where that side is indicated for convenience, shortness, or easy maintenance but it is preferable for other players in a match to be facing the player not behind him. If they have to cross the tee in order to take up that position so much more the wear caused.

These comments will apply equally to traffic areas round greens and between greens and tees with the addition that because they come into play, they will require extra thought and possibly a provision under local rules.

(i) Ladies
The green committee should include at least one representative from the Ladies Section because it is regretfully easy to discuss the play of a hole exclusively in terms of male requirements and indeed a hole must initially be designed for the male standard of scratch with local adjustments introduced into the pattern to accommodate both men and women who have less length or make more mistakes.

The reduction in distance for ladies tees is calculated by the Spanish Golf Federation as 15% and this is a useful guide, though the reduction should not be based on ultimate 'championship' lengths provided over about 6800 yards. A reduction of 15% on higher figures would bring the ladies tees in line with most of the men's ordinary tees and indeed these would be used for ladies championships. However, ladies' tee shots seem to be getting longer and the local L.G.U. representative is best qualified to advise.

In establishing ladies tees by measurements it is to be borne in mind that the L.G.U. requirements call for the stated distances to be taken from 'a selected point' on the tee not necessarily 2 yards from the back. (But equally to be marked with a permanent marker on the right hand side of the tee facing inwards.)

Where long carries over hazards lie in front of the tee it is normal to modify line as well as distance and the requirements of visibility may also affect the position since the principles involved

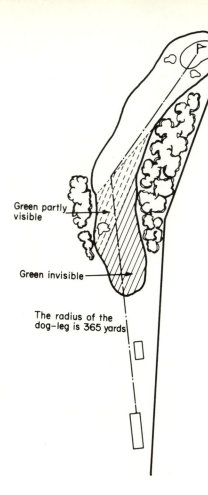

Green partly visible

Green invisible

The radius of the dog-leg is 365 yards

Fig. 4.4   The perfect dog-leg? No. 4 Royal Salisbury G.C. Zimbabwe, 495 yards, par 5.

are exactly the same. But where there is an extremely narrow gap between two bunkers, lady golfers have an unerring instinct for propelling their ball precisely through the middle of it. At short holes over 150 yards it may be wise to site the ladies tee to take advantage of this ability. The advantage of distance may be cancelled out by a less clear view of the hole or a sharp dog-leg at an awkward distance. The ladies' second shot, unless their tee is properly related to play, might equally be blind whereas male players see their objective clearly. Distance adjustment alone is not enough.

Wherever possible, it is desirable that the Ladies' tee should be out of danger from the Men's tee so that time is not wasted by the need for ladies to hang back in mixed matches till their partners have played.

(j) Mats, wear and repairs

In warmer climates, where growth is perceptible throughout the winter, and much stronger in summer, the condition of tees will inevitably be superior throughout the year and in winter no special measures will be needed.

In Britain, on many inland courses where drainage slows down as the soil reaches saturation from November onwards, depending on weather, it may be necessary to take regular tees out of use and use mats or some similar device.

Although recent developments have produced tee mats of artificial grass and nylon bristles (some of them very comfortable to play from), this recourse suffers from the fact that, in winter, mud from players' shoes will be tramped on to the tee mat and in the action of swinging, deposited on the surface. A close texture tends to hold the mud, to build up and become sealed. The use of nylon mats, therefore, only has marginal advantages over the coconut fibre mats formerly more common, though weight, 'playability' and appearance are certainly amongst them.

The more open, rubber-link tee mat suffers less in that respect and is to some extent self-cleaning if set on an open supporting base, though this cannot be so open or flimsy that a firm stance is inhibited. A concrete base should be perforated and set over a void. The purpose built wooden frames are slatted and weather resistant.

The siting of mats should be well away from grass tees because trampling round them churns any natural surface. Quite novel situations may be discovered between bushes or among trees which are possible because of the restricted point of departure. Indeed this novelty should be sought wherever possible because winter tee mats are unpopular and things which can be done to make them more interesting and acceptable are worth research. The ideal winter tee surface has still not arrived, but at least the expansion of the market has led to increased experiment and choice.

Where flat areas of grass cut at fairway length are available, e.g. on the paths sometimes mown through carry rough to reach the fairway or at the start of the fairway itself, these can serve for winter use and greatly ease shortage of teeing space of normal construction. Because they are at ground level and not specially prepared they will deteriorate more quickly, but, if extensive, frequent shifting of position will avoid severe damage. Again we see how superficial area is basic to year-round tolerance of play. Where new tees are concerned, the method of construction must be as advanced as the state of the art permits. It may be difficult at that early stage to provide the full area desirable, but if other factors conspire (traffic patterns, specifications, the levelling off of small areas of the early fairway or carry rough, maximum rotation) smaller areas may last through the winter in northern climates.

In warmer zones different considerations apply and change of tee position is generally limited to the coverage of the irrigation system. However, this facility coupled with sunshine, warmth and less intense use is likely to limit tee problems of wear to odd areas of shade from trees, poor surface drainage, or occasional disease.

It is also relevant that ground staff will often exceed twenty, permitting a degree of gardening likely, in winter, to please the eye of the golfer from further north.

Repair of damage will stop short of returfing whenever possible but recent developments in light turf rolls grown on a special medium can modify this attitude. This material roots quickly and the possibility of selecting new cultivars bred for their tough dwarf habits is attractive. But its freedom from unspecified grasses should be verified. Both for subsequent top-dressing and for the routine practice of filling divot marks with a mixture of soil and seed, the mixture should be moderately binding rather than pure sand. My father invented a 'divoting iron' which in essence was a hole cutter taking out a plug with egg shaped outline. This was used in earlier days for the instant repair of the line of a teeing off position during a competition. But such finesse is now hardly practical. Even so a 'patching iron', cutting a plug perhaps 9 inches in diameter is a useful tool in any greenkeepers' armoury for the quick removal of the occasional scorch due to spilt petrol, oil or chemical.

In general, all developing techniques for introducing seed superficially to reinforce a thin surface, for drainage without trenching or for improving irrigation are to be considered where shortage of space and labour have to cope with excessive play.

(k) The first tee

All the considerations discussed apply to the first tee, perhaps in greater measure, but there are additional points to observe if the player is to be put into the right frame of mind.

Firstly, it is customary to provide a larger teeing area so that wear will be really well distributed and the first impression of the course that much enhanced. Nairn has over 500 square yards of teeing space at no. 1 and the tee is always irreproachable.

The provision of permanent paths will, for the same reason, be obligatory with traffic further regulated by neat fencing and any necessary notices sited logically but discreetly and not at random. 'Crunchy' path surfaces are probably less desirable than firmer ones to avoid unexpected noise.

Its situation will be in view of the secretary's office and/or the professional's shop and the shop should be passed on the way to the first tee if it is not integral with the clubhouse.

Clearance of waste paper baskets should be a daily task incorporated in the routine of maintaining club-house surrounds.

All extraneous movement and noise from car park or supply vehicles should be obscured and muffled by planting or, better still, by additional mound work with integrating planting. The

Fig. 4.5   An elegant stone bridge spans the moat on the way to the 1st tee at St. Nom La Bretèche near Paris.

impression should be given that the world outside is shut off on the far side of the club-house. Here is a well tended, attractive golf course with a hint of excitement already in the overture. The curtain is about to go up on a game of golf which, whether it is the first on this course or one of thousands on this course, will definitely be unlike any other.

4.2   PUTTING GREENS

(a) Location: formation
There is no apparent justification for the level rectangular tee in the history of the game. Modern greens, on the other hand, have preserved their origins. When putting was less sophisticated than to-day, the green area was much smaller but none-the-less it would generally have been surrounded by the mounds, hollows and slopes which are inherent in modern design. On flat sites, reproducing this featuring today serves to fix the green in the landscape and give the climax of the hole some apparent purpose: on all sites, it adds to the interest of the shot following a near-miss of the green itself, through complication of stance, lie, and judgement. When new golf courses were made on links land, it was not unusual to site greens in hollows and, indeed, the fairways also automatically followed the comparatively level 'slacks'. Again the surrounds were anything but flat. Nor were they less varied when watering permitted elevated greens on links sites. Even the 'period' platforms constructed as greens inland were provided with marginal ridges and bumps which served the same purpose in a formal way.

Today, the fashion is to drag out the slopes of the surrounds to such a shallow grade that some of the fun implicit in more 'accidented' contouring has disappeared and we have moved further still in the opposite direction from the historical base from which we started. However, whether traditional, artificial, or merely elegant, the green design is made or marred by its location and the construction processes applied to it.

The layout planning process will, therefore, already have contributed in a strong measure to the design of the greens, because the selection of good green positions is the key which unlocks the true

(a)   (b)

Fig. 4.6   Two contrasting greens in the additional 9 holes at Portmarnock. (a) Narrow, with almost no entrance at the short, par 4, no. 4 in dune country. (b) Wider, but more bunkering on the approach to the flatter no. 7.

merits of the site. The contours of these positions must generally determine what design is most appropriate. Perhaps this is merely to say that the golf course architect of experience will discern the positions most desirable within his overall plan and know how best to profit from them while making the best of those which have to be accepted in the general interest and contrived wholly artificially.

The good green position will not always be dramatic. Quite small local contours may well provide the interest which the player is entitled to expect. Elsewhere a clump of trees or a stream bank may serve. All must be eventually controlled by the overriding need to grow good turf. A green in a frost hollow or enclosed by dense trees will always be a headache.

In all decisions there must be compromise between golfing needs, money, physical possibilities and landscape effect. Academic considerations might require a green to be formed wholly by 'cut' but bedrock is to be met 12 inches below the surface and an alternative site contains a fine clump of beeches. In practice this dilemma should never arise; it will have been resolved at the planning stage. Golf course layout is happily the most flexible of arts: its less obvious compromises can generally be pasted over and the others may produce what is sometimes loosely called 'character'. At the worst, that may be the best to be hoped for if the other seventeen holes are first class.

The situations and possible treatments which will be encountered can be categorized. The exercise is somewhat sterile but may help understanding and choice if the proper course of action is not immediately obvious, which it generally is.

1.	Rising Ground	Cut	Cut and fill	(Fill)
2.	Falling ground	—	(Cut and fill)	Fill
3.	Side slope	(Cut)	Cut and fill	Fill
4.	Brow/mound	Cut	Cut and fill	(Fill)
5.	Hollow	—	Existing levels Fill	
6.	Flat	—	Existing levels Fill	

The parentheses indicate comparative rarity and such operations are generally better avoided. Nevertheless, the designer of experience may choose what is unusual to heighten the drama of a particular location, where expense is not a primary consideration.

The method adopted will also determine the degree of visibility of the green surface and the emphasis on this provision is greater today than formerly. For example, other considerations apart, the green which is entirely built by cut into rising ground will be more likely to show some or all of its surface where the approach shot is played from below its level than if it were constructed entirely by fill. And the latter method on steeper slopes will lead to a high bank up to the front edge of the putting surface and some expensive problems in modelling the sides. Constructed entirely by 'cut', the putting surface will be at its lowest possible level but will be surrounded by inward slopes leading to the description: an 'armchair' green. It can even resemble a 'Wall of Death' (Woodbridge, no. 2).

On falling ground, if the descent is not too abrupt, some small measure of cut may be achieved at the front in order to reduce the build-up at the back although this should avoid the sort of gradient which causes the ball falling just short of the front edge (possibly unseen) to overshoot. But, generally at downhill holes, a green constructed by fill alone will be required and such greens unfortunately are the most difficult to render interesting.

On a side slope, visibility will again play an important role in the decision on form because where there is cut, the level will have to be extended forward on the cut side if the full entrance is to show. However, that is seldom essential and in any case, few greens are constructed on slopes strictly at right angles to the line of play because it is nearly always possible to orient the green to favour approach from one side of the fairway and fit the green into its slope, to some extent, diagonally. In general it is probable that the green made by cut and fill on a side slope will be more agreeable than one done purely by fill.

A green which straddles a ridge or a mound offers the same option, 'cut and fill' being the cheaper.

In a hollow or small valley either existing levels are possible or, if not, fill is inevitable. Equally, on flat ground the same options are available but there may be a greater tendency to build up greens for interest (and of course, drainage). Where this is done, the total effect should not seem repetitive (Krefeld) and it should not be exaggerated (Killarney).

In most cases, the cost of greens constructed purely by fill will exceed that of others because of the increased transport, although the quantities involved would be laughable to a motorway engineer. There are, however, other factors (extra topsoil strip and replacement, damage by traffic, compaction, access, restoration of borrow areas) which add to the expense and, on sites where existing grassland may be retained, to the damage done and the extent of restoration necessary. The West Lancashire Golf Club has, nevertheless, survived all these hazards of recent years and landscaped several areas both boldly and well.

Offers of free filling material for a new green are often made to golf clubs by firms needing to dispose of subsoil, or rubble. Such temptations should be treated with great caution. Detailed planning, traffic routes, control of material, removal and replacement of top soil (as well as price) must all be integrated and the timing co-ordinated with the golfing and greenkeeping calendar, the physical qualities of the course, and the potential employment of ground staff. Filling which contains large pieces of masonry or concrete should be avoided. Filling at the other end of the scale which may cause drainage problems should be treated with still greater reserve. Planning permission may be advisable.

It was suggested earlier that this part of the analysis of green construction might be considered sterile but it is intended primarily as a guide to those who have not done it before so that they may judge the effects of embarking on a particular line of action and because one still meets elementary errors. In practice, a contoured plan of the site with the contours of the new green imposed on it will demonstrate whether the further requirements still to be discussed can be satisfied or not. The experienced golf course architect will probably be able to estimate by eye whether the result of constructing any particular formation in any particular location is likely to be successful; those without experience should not proceed without a detailed plan to show that it can be done within the limits of purse, appearance and practicality.

(b) Area: dimensions
Having determined the optimum form of construction, there are other decisions to be taken before the detailed plan should be completed. These relate to putting area, internal falls, and the perimeter, closely allied to orientation and outline. In some measure these may be modified by the expected level of use and maintenance.

The dimensions of the putting surface will normally be related to the location of the green and the length and type of approach shot with the longer axis being generally (but not inevitably) on the line of the required approach shot. Without special reasons, the long axis should not be less than 25 yards and the short one, 14. With the front and back perfectly rounded, these measurements would produce a green of about 310 square yards. However, if the minimum distance of the hole position from the edge is taken as 5 yards, there would only be some 55 square yards available for cutting holes in a narrow strip down the centre of the green 4 yards wide by at the maximum, 15 yards. Adding 2 yards to the width increases the hole-cutting space to 85 square yards (35%) but the total

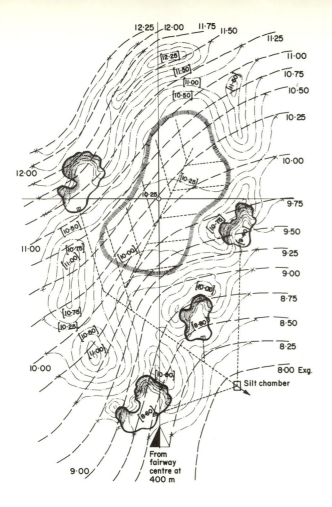

12·25 12·00 11·75 11·50
11·25
11·00
10·75
10·50
[12·25]
[11·50]
[11·00]
[11·50]
[10·50]
10·25
10·00
12·00
[10·25]
[10·25]
9·75
[10·75]
9·50
11·00
[10·50]
[10·75]
9·25
[11·00]
[10·00]
9·00
[10·00]
8·75
10·75
[8·80]
8·50
[10·25]
[10·50]
8·25
[11·00]
10·00
8·00 Exg.
[10·60]
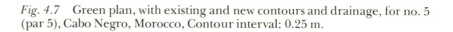
□ Silt chamber
[8·80]
9·00

▲

From
fairway
centre at
400 m

Fig. 4.7   Green plan, with existing and new contours and drainage, for no. 5
(par 5), Cabo Negro, Morocco, Contour interval: 0.25 m.

green area to 360 square yards (only 14%). Width is therefore more advantageous than length in improving holing space and reducing wear but has an important influence on play and must be correlated with perimeter outline and internal contour. It would, of course, be folly to combine these minimum dimensions in the same green but it would not be folly occasionally to make the transverse axis larger than the 'on line' measurement.

At the other end of the scale, the limit is only set by orientation, approach shot, grade on the putting surface, outline, and many factors of visibility and location. There are no precise rules to fetter experiment but the enthusiast would do well not to expect a generous response from players if both his surface grades and his outline are eccentric even though these will be more acceptable in a big area than a small one.

For practical purposes, one might take dimensions from 30 by 20 yards to 40 by 25 as the range within which to operate. These figures still leave scope for a noticeably smaller green or an even larger one when it is wished to create a strong effect and when there is logic behind the reasoning; for example, the retention of an important feature (the mound on the left of no. 4 in the new 9 holes, Portmarnock) or the enhancement of another (the amphitheatre of conifers filled by the 18th greens at Foxhills).

The relation of area to length of approach shot is still sometimes stated in simple terms – 'the shorter the approach, the smaller the green', as it was in the early days. It is doubtful whether any rule of golf course design can be so simple. It might be maintained for flat greens on flat sites but internal contouring and external contours must inevitably modify any judgement on what is an appropriate area. It will often be desired to introduce considerable rolls or different levels into the green of a hole of say 310 yards simply because it lacks distinction in other respects. Strong internal featuring restricts holing space considerably and automatically increases dimensions. Moreover it is not simply a matter of area. The general gradient on the putting surface could be zero or even front to back at a short par 4 whereas a long par 4 receiving a long shot might be tipped forward strongly at the shot. Area can only be a function of this type of decision.

Similar considerations arise at par 5 holes where again the approach shot should be a short one but, if the length is only 480 yards, may be the long iron of bigger hitters. Should the design compromise between the areas for the reception of no. 2 irons and 9 irons? Or should it select one of the others or modify this line of thought and seek interest and variety locally and in relation to the other holes in the round without strict observance of the rule?

The dilemma is often resolved by a form of words expressing the desirability of providing what is reasonable for the shorter hitter but 'tight' for the better player looking for a birdie, on the now familiar rationale that if he takes the risk it should be one which is calculated on the apparent hazards.

Holes strongly downhill may also require extra depth if considerations of contour, prevailing wind, and possible drought make the approach shot impossible in certain conditions. This sort of difficulty was once acceptable from time to time but is so no longer where the average golfer has produced an idea of the average course.

One situation in which area may be justifiably increased is at the 18th hole. To cite Nairn again, the 18th green has a fairly strong right to left slope but measures some 1130 square yards. This forms an impressive conclusion to a round, throws emphasis on to its very last strokes, and may just favour the cooler head and hand in a tight match.

Proximity to water will also mould the designer's decision on area. Where the penalty for failure to solve the problem set is absolute and involves restarting with another ball, it would be a stony heart that provided minimum landing area. There may be scope for such precise exercises in the higher professional tournament but no way of adjusting them for basic use. The repetitive use of water will be discussed elsewhere. It is enough here to say that, close to a green, it will be a dominating element in the design and a crucial test of the designer's compromises between art and difficulty in a deadly fashion. Proximity to other hazards has the same effect – rocks, quarries, sandpits or roads. Roads, however, in their most famous examples at the 17th holes at St Andrews and Hoylake are coupled with the contour and bunkering on the opposite sides of the greens to point their presence still more forcefully. The former is only 12 yards wide at the back and is generally uncomfortably angled to the approach shot even from a reasonable drive.

But one of the most photographed holes in the world, the short 7th at Pebble Beach, makes even less concessions. Perched on its rocky headland in the Pacific, it has a tiny area of some 200 square yards and width drops as low as 8 yards.

(c) Outline: orientation
The outline of the green's perimeter will generally produce narrower and broader sections of putting surface and will be derived from the wing bunkers and the mounded surrounds and slopes on the approach. These provide the general orientation but there is further scope for emphasis on 'target' areas curving out behind bunkers or even water. These bulges should not be so uncorseted that from some parts elsewhere on the putting area a ball can only be putted to the flag by going off the putting area. There will inevitably be someone who perversely takes a wedge to engineer this journey. Similarly, narrow tongues and salients no more than 10 yards wide will be largely wasted.

Marginal curves will be sinuous (or, as a French contractor once described it, 'Vénusien') so that mowing routine will be smooth. They will be related to the general formation on the encircling contours so that surrounds and putting surface form one coherent unit divided only by different heights of cut. Where this has been done properly, the tendency for day to day mowing to straighten out the sides should be resisted. The collar, where it is obvious, should be fairly uniform in width and not leave pockets whither the green was obviously designed to extend but does so no more. However, the truly fastidious (of whom Major Sarel, once secretary at The Berkshire was one), preferred their greens mown so that there was no apparent dividing line but only a gradual rise from putting length to surround length achieved by mowing outwards from the edge of the green while raising the mower blades by pressing on the handles – a hand machine, naturally.

Orientation is linked to the strategy built in to the design of the hole. The approach shot should benefit, if the drive has flirted with a bunker or other hazard and just slipped past or carried it, either by the avoidance of some further intermediate problem or by a more comfortable attack on the problems of the green itself. On the other hand, those who have played safe will find the orientation more disturbing especially if there is little room to stop the ball beyond a wing bunker.

Orientation will equally be brought into the scheme planned for dog-leg holes and may favour approach either from the short or the long way round.

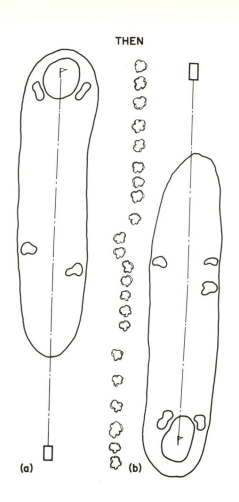

(a)   **(b)**

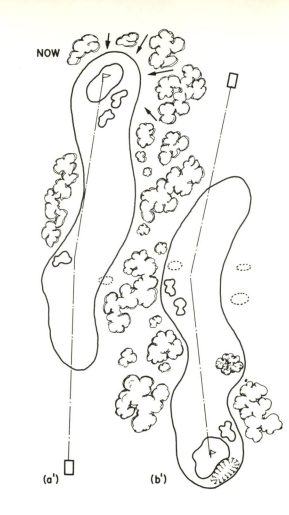

(a')   **(b')**

Fig. 4.8 'Then and now' diagrams do not mean much without contours, but this pair shows changes in style and attitude. Variations in fairway outline allows six bunkers to do more work than nine, formerly. The tree hazard in (b) shows the type of situation in which this might be used. But 'limb' it up to 10 ft so as not to obscure the green. Tree planting round green (a') and (b') helps to reduce the sense of parallel play – especially tiresome at consecutive par 4s, and still worse at consecutive par 5s.

As the length of par 4 holes drops, so the orientation may become more acute and the wing bunkers creep closer together and finally merge and surround the whole.

Steep surrounding contours will often determine orientation because, for example, a green in a strong rising slope may for practical reasons be built with its short axis nearly in line with play and the long axis across it. This device will generally be restricted to holes in the lower ranges of the relevant par. The bank beyond will permit some exaggeration of a short longitudinal axis but may lead to objections where balls hit thinly or too far, return to a favourable position on the putting green.

Orientation will also be related to the general fall on the green. In the example just quoted, a steeper forward facing slope on the putting surface might serve to mitigate a design offering minimal stopping distance for a shot from the designated line of play. Similarly a side slope which 'helps' a ball round to a target area fiercely defended on the direct line may offer the less skilful an option, and options, as we have seen, are the quintessence of golfing interest and ultimate satisfaction if their challenge is accepted and overcome.

At par 3 holes, green orientation will very often be at a greater or lesser angle to the line from the tee, the diagonal from left to right being probably more popular because the shot is easier and the ball stops more quickly. Depending on surface slope, the width can more easily be planned to be greater than the length because the approach is from a defined spot and this does not arise for all players at a par 4.

(d) Contouring: internal
Since 1945 it has been customary to provide the putting surface with a general fall from back to front. While this may inspire confidence in certain players it also has the effect of improving visibility and assisting estimates of the hole position.

Orientation and area, as we have seen, will be closely related to gradient but practical factors of drainage cannot be ignored. Many greens, poorly constructed from the greenkeeping standpoint, remain playable because surface water can be shed, throwing less work on the soil structure to

Fig. 4.9   Early 20th century featuring by Willie Park Jnr. at Huntercombe. Originally an estate development, the only house built lies beside this green. (Courtesy of M.G. Hawtree.)

remove surplus moisture. Similarly it would be undesirable on the face of it to leave a green cut into a slope with a fall towards the 'cut side'. The general surrounding surface flow must be respected, however adequate the drainage and specification.

A general gradient also assists the provision of an adequate drainage system below the top soil. It is customary to specify a fall on green drains of 1 in 100 thus, if the surface gradient is the same, an even depth is retained. On a level green the depth would increase towards the front and raise the cost of further excavation for drains external to the green system unless the whole surface has been elevated above the surroundings.

The other end of the normal run of gradients lies around 1 in 60 but locally can be increased to 1 in 40. After that the slope becomes limited if there is risk of a ball accelerating to finish inevitably beyond the desired goal en route. This is simply another way of saying that rolling greens and fast greens need a greater area, not only for finding adequate nearly level space to cut holes, but also to offer a braking area to putts negotiating acute slopes. A totting-up process has to be applied to the design to strike an average gradient. We may recall Tom Simpson's advice which would limit undulations to 25% of the surface.

In countries where winter frosts discolour the Cynodon or Bermuda Grass greens necessary for summer heat, the gradients and rolls may have to be very tentative to suit the glossy surface which develops as the blades yellow and desiccate. Happily, the inimitable Penncross Bent has gone some way to removing this limitation which can otherwise only be overcome by techniques of oversowing differing species for winter and summer or further experiment with the dwarf strains of rye-grass.

Moulding the putting area is probably the most difficult feature to achieve successfully by artifice, just as the shots eventually performed on it are the most delicate of all. Our forefathers who selected a piece of ground in which to place a hole were not worried by elaborate preparations with drainage, stone layers, and soil mixes which today generally precede the final modelling of the putting surface. Their contouring came ready-made. It is nearly always true that some degree of borrow will appear in any area raked out by eye. Thus our first ploy is to put away the level once the general surface grades designed have been established and the pegs have been put in to fix the specified depths of the stone layer, if provided, and the topsoil.

The purists require that the foundation or stone layer should reproduce or echo the contouring to be provided on the final surface. In a general sense this is obviously desirable. In practice, any early attempts at subtlety will be lost unless the construction processes are executed with a good deal of expensive manipulation. Moreover, in northern climates, the dry spells of summer are generally short and a programme involving the construction of a full eighteen holes is not only interrupted by rain, but often suffers from a late start due to official planning processes, committees and financial clearance; in Scotland particularly, local summer holiday periods are observed and the plant may be pulled off the site for two weeks. Delays are in fact endemic in the whole operation and they are not helped by the fact that operations extend over more than 100 acres and that a ring watermain probably has to be installed during the same period.

This recital is less a complaint than a warning that the ultimate refinements we have sometimes discussed throughout this section will be extremely difficult to achieve within certain time scales, climates and soil conditions. One will aim at the ideal, but be obliged by events to fall short of it. It will be possible to do the job right, but very often it could have been 'righter'.

Thus any subtle contouring to be introduced deliberately is more likely to be restricted to the final operation on the green surface. Big features within the putting area must obviously be provided for from the foundation up; but the more subtle gradations will be executed in the topsoil not by reducing its depth, but by adding to it.

The most obvious device (and perhaps the most common because the most obvious) is the green built on two levels. The intermediate slope should not be so steep that mowing scalps the brow. The area of the green will be increased proportionately because some 200 square yards of holing space will be deducted from the potential.

The front lower section must also be big enough and at such a gradient that any acceleration of the ball passing down the slope can be contained. One has seen putts on the 1st green at St Andrews which sent the ball back into the Swilken Burn, but the first club playing over this course was formed in 1754 and so a great many things may be forgiven.

The intermediate change of level should, in any event, be well dragged out for appearance as well as maintenance and preferably fit at either side into some related featuring of the surrounds.

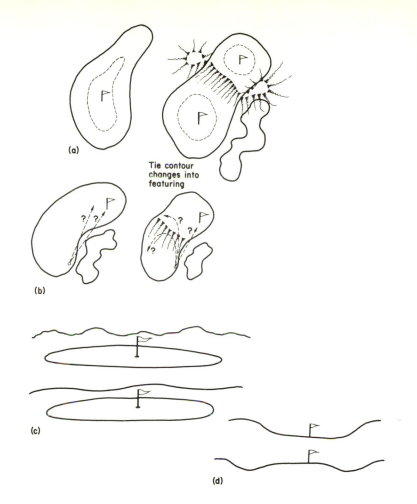

Fig. 4.10 Some green memories. (a) Thin greens and salients reduce putting area. Large internal contour changes demand a greater area. (b) Exaggerated bean shapes limit acceptable hole positions. Still more so with heavy surface contouring. (c) TOP: Too much feature in too short a distance; BOTTOM: Smoother moulding is better. (d) TOP: 'Armchair' comfort; BOTTOM: More work but less 'upholstery'.

The device can often be employed usefully at short par 4s or at par 5s which may lack other interest. An undemanding approach shot can be spiced by the extra calculations and possibilities which this design presents, especially where the bank is properly angled rather than wrongly presented at a right-angle.

This design is also very useful in greens built into rising ground because less excavation is required and the front slope up to a cut and fill green is reduced. There is even scope for three levels where the rise is steep, though other difficulties may then arise because total area is inflated again.

Chief among these is the question of visibility. A semblance of visibility may be achieved by showing the intermediate bank where the two level areas are otherwise above the player's line of sight and thus not seen. Where the elevation is not too severe the player will still be able to estimate the position of the hole but where the whole of the formation is unseen, estimates of which level contains the hole may become a gamble. When that happens the player will feel cheated. This problem is overcome at the 16th at Tandridge, a Colt course near Oxted in Surrey, by using two flags on the flag stick for one level and one flag for the other. The purist will not approve but it is salutary to give him scope to express his views.

(e) Contouring: external

The need for featuring whether artificial or natural, to surround the putting surface has been noted as part of the historical approach to the game and the interest of playing today. It relates the putting surface to the surrounding contours and creates the illusion of a natural conclusion to the hole. Large parts of Galloway in the south west of Scotland are so shaped that it would only be necessary to position the flags to provide a simple 18 holes and this prompts the thought that perhaps our inland featuring overemphasizes its seaside origins. It is certainly very easy to exaggerate the ups and downs. If there is too much variation in a small distance the effect can be as disagreeable as poor grades on banks or no elaboration at all.

Tom Simpson recommended 1 in 4 as a general rule for grading featuring with 1 in 3 behind greens. This was the first attempt to define what was proper but may have been partly guided by

Fig. 4.11   The last green of Killarney's original 18 uses the lake and pine trees effectively, but others are artificially elevated. (H.W. Neale, Action Photos.)

the mechanical equipment available. Modern machines shift great volumes of soil very readily and the tendency has been to produce even smoother grades, 1 in 6 or 1 in 7, to the point where the merging of featuring becomes unseen as it should be, but losing some of the identity of the featuring itself.

The natural slopes round greens on links land will often be steeper and 1 in 3 or 1 in 2 will not be unusual. But these gradients are on infertile sand where tussocks of fescue, ground willow, and marram grass are typical and indeed essential to maintain any kind of cover. But such natural cover has been accepted for centuries and it requires only minimal maintenance. Inland, the rough which would develop in slopes of this sort would not be acceptable and therefore they have to be cut – an awkward tedious job on anything much steeper than 1 in 4 and easy and agreeable on 1 in 5 and 1 in 6 with a wide choice of ride-on machines to effect it.

Now, taking 1 in 5 as our norm, we can return to the elaboration of featuring and the warning that too much variation in elevation in too short a distance produces a fussy unnatural appearance. A mound 3 feet high will obviously require 30 feet in profile at the base to slope up to the top and back to ground level at 1 in 5. But no mound can be formed so exiguously and with a gently rounded top and perhaps a dip to vary one of the side slopes it is more likely to require a base of 45 feet at least. Thus if the rules of gradient are observed and featuring is tolerably bold, the mounding of the green surround will automatically adjust to the broad scale required.

Next the height of mounds introduced in the featuring must clearly vary in order to avoid any apparent artificiality and it is likely that the higher features will look best towards the back of the green rather than too early in the design. Thus, on level ground, a series of three mounds 3 feet, 2 feet, and 4 feet in height would extend over some 130 feet on plan, more than the length of the side of the average green and therefore already covering part of the back. If the dips between mounds sweep below the putting surface level then clearly the extent of this series will be that much longer.

Featuring is not always moundwork. The banks of greens made partly in cut must be modelled in the same way – for example the top edge of the cut can be raised and brought back to existing contours further up the slope after forming a shallow trough. This device not only enhances the modelling but also has an important role to play in planning the disposal of any surface water

Fig. 4.12   Minimum elevation provides visibility and stopping space at no. 12 green (west), Le Prieuré, near Paris. (Courtesy of George Wilson.)

otherwise likely to arrive on the green itself. This is an essential study in areas of high rainfall or sudden torrential storms. Catchwater or French drains with stone up to the surface are better on roadside embankments than in green surrounds but may well prove necessary even below quite small slopes created artificially. Nevertheless the moulding of the land above the sides and backs of new greens should collect and lead away heavy rainfall by creating suitable swales which will deposit it outside play or where appropriate in a pool created as reservoir or hazard or both. This provision is particularly important at courses staging important tournaments which could be held up by heavy rain lying long after the storm has passed, even on new courses with free-draining mixtures on greens, if the storm is torrential.

The sum total of all these operations should leave a land-form which the eye can follow appreciatively as it curves gently up and down in elevation and to and fro on plan with no part of it echoing another either in height or shape and the whole sitting easily in the landscape as if it had always been there. Even the bunkers, though sand will be foreign to the majority of sites, can be made to look as if a fortunate seam of sand ran naturally and very conveniently across the approach to the green and their faces and shapes will be moulded appropriately into the featuring itself.

Where the designer is really in a corner and obliged to make a green, on a mountain course for instance, where the slope on the site simply does not permit the grading which he would like, he can sometimes resort to the use of bunkering to enable a 1 in 2 sand face to gain him a little more space for a 1 in 4 grass slope elsewhere.

In searching for some rationale, historically or philosophically, for contouring the putting surface in newly constructed greens, the surrounding featuring will certainly provide an initial departure point. Mounds can be continued into, say, the first five yards of the putting surface itself and hollows, the same. Thus the design of the green in plan and in section becomes a unit all the way from its centre to surrounding, undisturbed ground in any direction.

The two-tiered green, as already mentioned, demands the provision of a landscaping reason, artificial or otherwise, for the division between the two tiers and, as we saw, this division itself must be formed with subtlety and not as a mere step. The rolling green may justifiably become smoother towards the centre or, in another case, towards the centre of the areas defined and separated by contouring. Historically this basis is acceptable and indeed more so than the smooth plane tilting towards the shot which other considerations may introduce.

But finally there is a totally random element which can or even should be introduced because there are totally random contours in most greens which have survived a hundred years or more. It is not too much to guess that the Green Convener of 1750 selected a green site because it was not flat. With the style of putting and the adventurous attitude of golfers then performing, why should it be? The danger of analysing golf course architecture lies in categorizing and hence distorting its central thesis. There is always another answer which may be almost as good.

(f) Stock types
From all these considerations of construction and landscaping only seven named types of green have emerged, and they are all exceptional:

The *island* green speaks for itself. Recent developments of golf architectural fashion in the United States have led to a conscious search for individuality and it is not uncommon to see new greens entirely surrounded by sand or water. The sand surroundings have obvious problems in upkeep, while an island green in water, though pretty, may unduly depress too many golfers. There is, nevertheless, a sense in which an heroic hole of this type may inspire or fascinate the player, even if it causes him to lose several golf balls.

The *plateau* green, totally elevated above its surroundings, is, as we saw earlier, helpful for drainage in flat sites, and also for giving some climax to the hole in land otherwise unremarkable. Unfortunately, it has a tendency to resemble others and it is difficult to introduce significant variety.

The *punch-bowl* green, the opposite of the plateau, was not uncommon in the earlier days of siting greens on links or heathland, because it provided a built-in automatic watering system, and the grass stayed greener in summer. There are still a few examples about, but as traffic increases, rainfall tends to remain longer on the surface and day to day use is too restricted. Lobbing the ball into the bowl with the expectation that it must finish somewhere near the hole also tends to pall very quickly.

From time to time, where changes are in the air, a Green Convener will be asked to consider the possibility of a *double green*. The antecedents of this formation are obviously impeccable and its comparative rarity outside the Kingdom of Fife make it, superficially at least, an attractive proposition. However, the circumstances which permitted or indeed obliged the double green to be provided at 14 holes at St Andrews could seldom be repeated elsewhere.

They grew out of the original double use of nearly all intermediate greens and it is generally overlooked that they depend absolutely on size and the opposite polarity of the axis of the related holes. A plan which tries to repeat this type of circuit on anything but a linear site runs into great problems and is wasteful of acreage. On existing courses a move in this direction should only be made if the greens are back to back, an element which is sometimes overlooked. A double green for two parallel holes can only be achieved if the green width is approaching 100 yards. That is to say, a great deal of effort will go into the maintenance of the central 50% of the putting surface with no corresponding benefit to play or condition. Certainly this width can be slowly reduced as the angles of approach increasingly diverge but safety and the avoidance of interference demand the same respect as in more normal formations.

Another possible obstacle is that of circulation. Two greens back to back effectively seal off lateral traffic other than over a playing surface. This may cause difficulties in maintenance and where the layout is convoluted.

Where the double green can be achieved in front of the club house at 9 and 18 there are many additional factors to commend it. The size will be appropriate, the interest from the club house ideal and the generous proportions (being marginal in the layout) less restrictive on the plan as a whole. The size will also permit more vigorous contouring which again may be considered appropriate at this point of the round.

Even so the location of 1st and 10th tees may cause circulation problems and there are those who disapprove an arrangement where progress from the 9th green to 10th tee involves walking past the 18th causing some degree of disturbance or delay.

The *two-level* green with two distinct levels has become known as a 'Mackenzie' green. In fact, he had no original claim to this conventional type which is still very much in vogue. The true

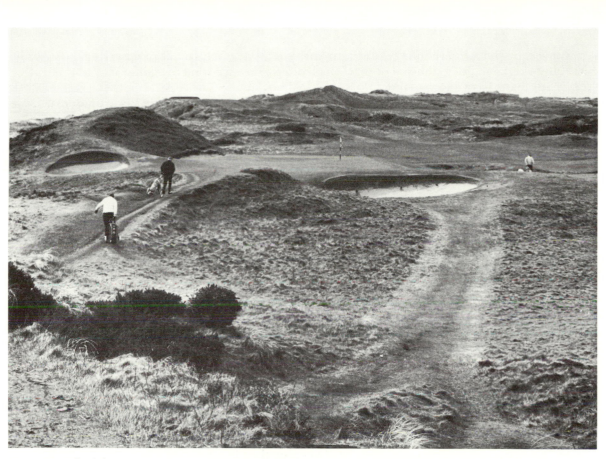

Fig. 4.13   The 8th (postage stamp) green at Troon, seen from the tee. Length, 126 yards. (H.W. Neale, Action Photos.)

'Mackenzie' green had, certainly, two or more different levels, but they were separated by slopes not generally at right angles to the line of play which often exceeded what the golfer may tolerate as 'fair'. Thus many have disappeared.

The *armchair* green, as we saw, appears where the green is built in 'cut' and inward slopes occur at the back and sides. Favourable results from deliberate use of the slopes in approaching the hole are not necessarily a bad thing but bunkering and hollows at the feet of the slopes need careful calculation to ensure that a fair deal is accorded to the precise player.

The *pocket handkerchief* or *postage stamp* green explains itself. The considerations discussed under area must be carefully weighed against the value of shock tactics and future upkeep problems because the location, which may often seem to justify this choice, is probably itself already exaggerated.

Specials – There is no reason why the surface should not be split into three levels if the site requires it, but the use of the sub-level system to overcome lateral slope is not to be recommended. There is, or was, a short hole at St Cloud which had the intermediate bank running in the same axis as the shot. Although perfectly visible, the halving of width is uncomfortable and flukey.

Very occasionally the back section of a green is made lower than the front providing a sharp forward propulsion to the shot which pitches on the intermediate section. The rarity of this formation indicates what players' reaction is likely to be.

The 7th green on the Wentworth West Course probably represents the ultimate in the two level concept. In the Ryder Cup in 1953, one American player took four putts. Failing to breast the big rise from the front level with his first putt, the possibility of three more putts was always present. And so it turned out. (Even unhappier things occurred there in October, 1982.)

The vast majority of putting greens are, however, *anonymous*. That is how it should be. Recognizable types should only appear where there are particular reasons either of bad contour or of continuing interest and pressure at a particular part of the round. It would generally be a mistake to pull a design off the shelf and apply it to a new situation without going through all the premeditation necessary if one is to be sure of keeping the silent majority silent.

The general alignment of the green, its perimeter, its dimensions, its orientation, its internal slopes are ultimately a blend of ingredients which will taste different according to wind, weather and line of approach. The confection will not shock the palate if the thinking has been right before the shot, and the body produces the movements expected of it. Essentially, the good green design will continue the same process of selecting options which begins on the tee and only ends when the ball disappears into the hole. There is simply no standard pattern of priorities in design to produce this effect.

4.3   BUNKERS

Apart from grass and contour (in other words, the site itself modified for golf) there are only three design elements available for the golf course architect – sand, trees, and water; and the greatest of these is sand. Its landscape effect is instantaneous; it proclaims the golf course and breaks up its units into subsidiary proportions like the glazing bars of a Georgian window. It will do neither of these things unless it is mostly well seen. On links land the need for preservation from wind erosion tends to keep sand areas low, the golf course may well proclaim itself without visible sand. The dark shadows of hollows and banks in the softer undulations of fairways outline the bare facts and the imagination soon does the rest. Inland, sand defines and emphasizes a fairway, a green, a feature, and even modifies the landscape within the fairly big acreage to which it is relevant.

Sand bunkers affect the golfer positively or negatively. Positive bunkers influence the player before playing a shot, causing him to select a certain line, a certain type of shot to essay a certain carry, or to play deliberately short but generally to cause him to think his play right through from tee to green. Negative bunkers are those which do not enter into this thought process because they merely affect a bad shot and are punitive rather than provocative. All this has been said many times before but being at the basis of an important part of the game, it needs to be sketched in again before moving on.

Bunkers left and right of the fairway seemingly indicate the desirability of a central line of play which on the whole is the least interesting. If, in fact, the optimum line passes close by or over one of them then the other one is not constructive and has to be justified on other grounds rather than playing effect.

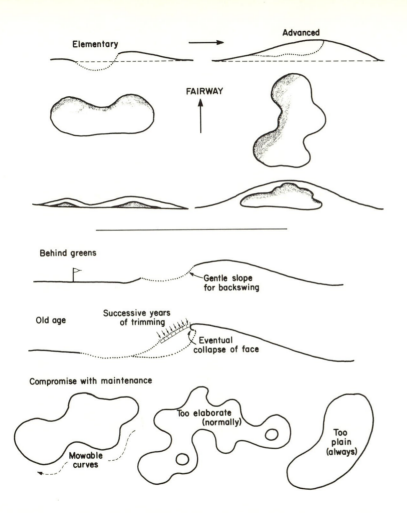

Elementary

Advanced

FAIRWAY

Behind greens

Gentle slope
for backswing

Old age

Successive years
of trimming

Eventual
collapse of face

Compromise with maintenance

Too elaborate
(normally)

Too
plain
(always)

Mowable
curves

Fig. 4.14 Bunkers.

Fig. 4.15　No bunkers at all at the 4th green, Lindrick. It is, in fact, out of sight from the fairway. Called the Cockpit, from an earlier sport when hopping over the nearby county border was sometimes advisable to escape the law. (H.W. Neale, Action Photos.)

In the Fifties and Sixties many clubs found themselves with a legacy of a hundred or more bunkers because successive generations had added new ones further on without filling old ones further back. But the reduction of ground staff for economy had to be matched by a stream-lining process in which superfluous bunkers were the first to be axed and the likely reasonable total today is about 70.

Where old bunkers are filled in there is much to be said for doing no more than remodel the bank and old sand area to mowable contours while retaining something of the old mound and hollow. It is important that the hollow should not be left in a form which tends to collect golf balls in one area leading to a concentration of divots, but otherwise this small echo of golf's origins will do no harm, especially round greens. Similar considerations apply to the creation of new grass bunkers which might be considered where visibility of the sand is absent. It is disagreeable to find a ball on a patch of earth excavated by localized divot marks.

The most valuable import from the USA of recent years has been the refurbished concept of the fairway bunker all raised above ground and lying parallel to the play. This has several advantages. The sand area is well seen and much more of it is seen than in a transverse, partly hollowed bunker where only the face is likely to be visible, and sometimes only part of the face. The absence of drainage problems will be welcome and the entry, exit, and use of the small machines designed to rake the sand is facilitated.

The long axis lying parallel to play will often permit a longer recovery shot than from sand areas dominated by a steep bank towards the green. Without arguing the desirability or otherwise of this characteristic, one can at least say that a good recovery after error is more stimulating than compounding error with frustration.

Lastly, the landscape effect of a deeper bunker, even a large one, is often reduced to nothing from a distance or to no more than a thin bar of sand in the distance which lacks any character. The built-up design seems to be much more flexible and to display its formation to advantage from a distance. This factor may lead to the excessive elaboration and repetition in what have been called 'Mickey Mouse' bunkers.

The thoughtful Green Committee will doubtless restrain a greenkeeper or contractor whose

Fig. 4.16   Moor Park, to show the original Twenties bunkering style at no. 3. (H.W. Neale, Action Photos.)

(a)

Fig. 4.17 The High course no. 12 at Moor Park. (a) 1954 (Flory van Donck in play), (b) now. The cross bunker evidently failed to please. Note also how the later bunker outlines have been simplified and seem to have produced some problems with the face of the nearest one at least. Tree growth and natural regeneration behind the green are also interesting. (H.W. Neale, Action Photos.)

(b)

enthusiasm for the new form carries him too far away from the general character of his course. It is clear, however, that increase of size which is the only way to get away from the basic form of transverse bunkers leads to less visual benefits than equivalent elaboration at a higher level.

The bunker set into a mound is, of course, no novelty to British design but it has generally been recommended exclusively for clay sites where drainage problems would otherwise arise. It can be used far more widely to advantage and apart from drainage benefits, there can be others – avoidance of stone, of subsoil working up through the sand, of chalk, in fact of many of the ailments to which excavated bunkers are subject. Indeed the problem of draining an excavated sand area is not always one to be lightly solved and unless there is a direct outlet (itself, not without further problems), evacuation of rain or irrigation water will always take longer.

The standard British inland bunker tends to be built more or less transversely to the line of play with a tongue breaking the face near the middle and a corresponding dip in the bank behind. It is 10–12 yards wide and 4–5 yards in breadth. On Colt courses round Birmingham (Edgbaston, Copt Heath, Harborne) bunkers tend to be bigger and of more interesting form because Colt, as we read, selected his positions as much from the lie of the land as from arbitrary considerations of distance and this helped him to build more freely. Courses on the Bagshot sands in Surrey permitted more imaginative treatment and sand areas were still more variously and prettily formed.

The 'design and construct' firm of Hawtree and J.H. Taylor engaged several Irish foremen in the Twenties: Regan, Ryan, Brick among them, who had a great gift for the delicate art of outlining a sand area to make it attractively natural. Ryan was thought to go a little too far in his lace-edged intricacies, but this was probably no bad thing in those days when hand labour in maintenance was the rule and when future greenkeepers will, in any case, tend to trim off excrescences which unduly complicate their routine. At Royal Birkdale, the foreman was Gillett who came from those parts. Unfortunately, many of his bunkers were transformed on the Scottish model for practical considerations by the R & A Championship Committee.

This style, modified from the links model, where it has been taken inland, faces the bunker with turf or peat-bricks, on which grass grows above the sand line. This permits a much steeper face and the bunkers at Muirfield have become legendary. Indeed, the exactitude with which good players

Fig. 4.18   Herbert Fowler liked the cross-bunker, especially at no. 18, as at Walton Heath.

splash the ball from shallower sand bunkers may demand a response on those lines. It is a question now not of whether the expert player gets down in two but whether he holes it. But grass-faced bunkers have certain objections in appearance and, if they suffer in drought, parts may break up. This is particularly likely to happen where a hover-mower is used to trim the grass face and dry weather follows.

Indeed, the whole treatment of bunker faces has to be related to the site and the style of maintenance. The grass face has become part of the scene on many Scottish golf courses even inland where the problems of erosion and wind blow are absent. Because the Scots must know best, the practice has become acceptable and entered into the vernacular.

Elsewhere the problem is rather different. Where sand is taken up the faces it has to be repeatedly pushed back even to its usual angle of repose. This used to be done by reversing the rake when raking the floor from the inside of the bunker. Where bunker raking machines are used, raking sand back up the face is done from outside, with the teeth of the rake. Less sand is brought up and the lip may start to break away. A similar lack of sand eventually produces the overhanging lip of bunkers, especially on heather courses.

Some of these difficulties spring from a reluctance to top up the floor with new sand. The natural process of deepening is so gradual that its effects precede detection and the remedy is sought in some other direction.

All styles, apart perhaps from the shallow dish, produce maintenance tasks, sometimes disproportionate to their advantages. Suggestions for more bunkers should, therefore, be carefully related to the current success of the hole concerned and the possibility of a corresponding reduction at another point. If everything else is right, fairly sparse bunkering can still give the landscape effect and playing interest which may be lacking in an area unadorned.

The pot bunker was essentially of seaside origin and does not transfer happily inland. On links courses it was, and is, often used in clutches of three in line ahead to cover a wider area without the sand blow which would affect one larger sand bunker.

The bunkering of a hole is not something taken out of a pattern book and selected in preference to others. It is dictated by the total topography of the hole in which the possible formations of the

Fig. 4.19   Sand, lake, fountain, palm trees, mountains and golf at La Manga. The wing bunker at the green shows how the desire for easy maintenance leads to oversimplified, unnatural form. (H.W. Neale, Action Photos.)

green are vital but not necessarily dominating. A green which has to be oriented in one particular axis will dictate the best line of approach which in turn will generate the wing bunkering at the green and thence the basic bunkering system to be elaborated according to fairway slopes, dog-leg angle, and so on. Once an individual element in a hole is extracted and discussed in isolation we are already distorting its appreciation.

Wing bunkering is most likely to fulfil our standards of positive effect and forward planning. It interacts vigorously with hole position and is more or less fearsome according to the length of the hole and the success of the drive.

There is a tendency to plan wing bunkers further out than formerly in order to eliminate hand work on a narrow collar and avoid wear which concentrated traffic would produce. Orientation, therefore, has to be rather more exaggerated by the wing bunkers in order to produce the same demands on the approach shot which are presented by bunkers tight to the green.

Throughout this discussion I have avoided the use of the word 'trap'. This always seems to me an unworthy slur on the designer's intentions. As J.L. Low said 'Let BUNKERS more perfectly abound'.

4.4   FAIRWAYS AND ROUGH

The greater part of the golf course is often left to its own devices. Indeed there are not a great many ways, outside the appropriate maintenance, to improve the design of the fairways and the rough. Nevertheless, it may be useful to consider them here.

A broad fairway is 50 yards wide, a narrow one, 25. In practice 35 to 40 yards is a useful average. This leaves scope for variation in outline which is particularly desirable at holes where the tee is at a higher level and the whole fairway visible.

The pattern could provide a comfortable width of 45 yards at 150 yards from the tee, 40 at 200, 35 or 30 at 250. Metrically, allow 40 m at 140 m from the tee, 35 at 180, and 30 at 230 m. But these widths should not be provided by simply tapering the margins. These should oscillate in and out on a broad wavelength. Fairway centres should not be closer to each other than 70 yards at critical

Fig. 4.20   Trees in variety of form, height and colour embellish this fairway at Auckland, New Zealand.

points, so even the wide section will still leave 25 yards ($12\frac{1}{2}$ + $12\frac{1}{2}$) of rough to the fairway of a parallel hole and, as the two wide sections seldom coincide, generally rather more. In this extreme case, there is not much space for the deeper rough which can follow the usual marginal bands of semi-rough so it will probably not appear. In any case the full 25 yards will be very much in play from both directions. But those marginal bands besides extracting some degree of penalty and providing shot-variety show an intermediate length between short fairway and the full rough where this is allowed to grow. This intermediate length can be 5 or 10 yards wide or, on public courses, endless, but hay-length grass directly against the fairway looks artificial and wrong. As with tree planting, sharp divisions and edges are to be avoided.

Once a pattern has been established it is not an easy matter to preserve it. There are two irresistible tendencies when driving a tractor or ride-on mower. One is to straighten things up: the other is to nibble off a little bit more especially round greens where a neat finish is important. In fact the sharp cut down from collar length to putting green length generally produces a leafless stalky strip which looks worse than an equivalent width uncut.

Thus, every so often, fairway and green outlines should be reviewed to make sure they have not all straightened out or expanded. Dog-legs should also be checked to make sure they have not become more human in appearance.

An aerial photograph or plan prepared from an aerial survey is particularly useful in analysing what might be done to improve fairway outlines and in the otherwise difficult task of defining the modifications required. This will also help to decide which features (trees, shrubs, bunkers, ponds, hollows) could be usefully and attractively brought into the fairway by modifying the mowing outline. They will be much more effective when distinguished in this way and the fairway can be adjusted to emphasize them further.

There are rather more things that can be done to the outer rough, one of the most important being to do nothing at all. On many sites simple neglect will permit natural regeneration to produce hawthorns, oaks, ash and many more trees and shrubs depending on the nature of the site. Because of fire hazard, this type of treatment should not be continuous and it is seldom in any case that the acreage will be great enough to permit that luxury. But small plots can be selected to either side, for

Fig. 4.21   Rough country on the right limits bunkering needs at no. 11, Royal Birkdale.

example, of the carry rough, and by identifying a particular area, they will limit the search for a ball as well as adding welcome features cheaply.

The carry rough is generally fairly clear of taller obstacles except at short holes and its extent from the tee is normally of the order of 100 to 120 yards. 150 yards is too long (see Appendix 1) except from a tee only used by experts.

Often an existing feature can be retained in the carry rough and specially maintained as a hazard – a hedge corner as at the 12th at Prestbury, pollarded oaks forming a carpet of branches below the elevated short hole tee of no. 8 at Ghent (Les Buttes Blanches), beneath which one walks from the tee to the green as through a mature nuttery. In case the purist finds it difficult to square this with the doctrine of informality on the golf course, one should add that this hole is right by the club house where a modicum of ornament may be accepted.

4.5   TREES

Introducing new trees to a golf course is one of the simpler tasks of the Green Convener and where discretion is exercised it is likely to receive universal approbation. Even if he does no more than initiate a programme, fund it, and implement its first stages, he will have made a significant contribution to his golf course.

Ideally, tree planting should form part of the original concept of the golf course layout. Trees may even be essential to full and interesting use of the ground. But they should not be relied on too soon as a safety factor, either present or future, even though a good plan will use existing trees as strategic playing features. Planting is a very useful addition to the designer's limited armoury.

Once established, the correct varieties need little upkeep, but it is essential to order the right varieties. The Forestry Commission is not necessarily the best source of advice because they deal with a different type of culture, but they can certainly lay down broad lines. A landscape architect or good local nurseryman should always be consulted in preparing the planting list, establishing availability, and advising how and when to plant.

There is often some scope for planting new trees to improve playing interest. Trees situated in

Fig. 4.22   Diagonal cross bunkers in plenty under the second shots at 17 and 18, Sunningdale, Old Course. (H.W. Neale, Action Photos.)

Fig. 4.23 Trees.

Fig. 4.24 The 12th hole on the Longcross course of the Foxhills Country Club. The trees narrow down the fairway for longer drives. Bunkers set in the rising ground show up from the tee and drain easily. (Courtesy of Foxhills Country Club.)

fairways will generally be older than the golf course, unless subsequent shifts of tees or greens have made use of planting which was marginal when the course began. It is not customary to plant a new tree within a fairway except occasionally as a future replacement for an existing favourite whose life, lightning or golf balls are likely to abbreviate. But the possibility is by no means to be excluded, especially at dog-legs.

In principle, a tree hazard can be used exactly as a sand bunker in defining line. But discretion will temper its distance in order to limit the number of players whose best drive or second shot will finish just behind it. In any case it is effective over a much wider area and far more interesting when it modifies but does not block a fair shot.

All successful shots in golf are satisfying if they produce the carefully planned result. But there may be a bonus in the one which sails over trees, not only exactly on target, but also on the projected trajectory. If the alternative line is optional then blindness is permissible; if it is obligatory, a thin screen can be allowed to obscure some of the air-space on the way to the green, but not the green itself. This is both decorative and stimulating. The not-too-long short hole is very suitable for this device, often found on courses carved out of pine woods, like Pals on the Costa Brava. This is also the type of hole where the idea can be developed on existing courses by allowing small trees in the carry rough to creep up imperceptibly into view and eventually into play. The conspiracy must obviously be communicated from one chairman to the next.

Most tree-planting programmes will be restricted to the margins. A course with every hole completely isolated from the others is ideal. Unfortunately, many inland courses, especially round big cities, are laid out on closely parallel lines for maximum length and economy of land use. This may not allow enough width between fairways for any considerable density. Here it is much better to abandon the idea of total separation and plant as thickly as possible in areas where the fairway can be waisted, connecting the groups with isolated specimens. A thin single line does not enhance the landscape, but lateral views and vistas between groups will give added merit to groups concentrating interest on the hole itself.

Free spaces are still more important round greens for air drainage. Trees planted as background to greens receive approbation except from certain 'links-eyed' purists but if planting is carried

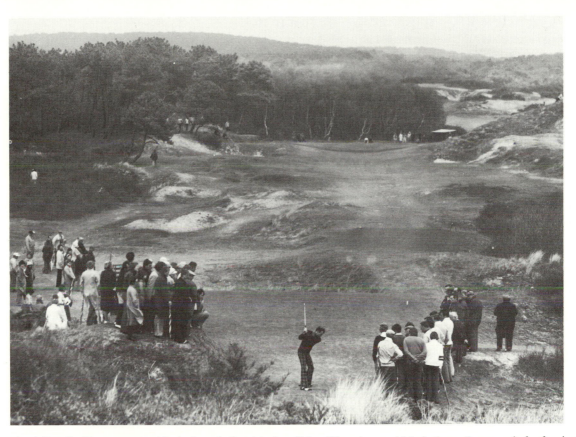

Fig. 4.25 Le Touquet, no. 15. A short hole with simplicity. The pine and birch decor is not strictly classical, but very acceptable. (H.W. Neale, Action Photos.)

round the sides it should still provide channels for air to move across the surface, drying off dew, and reducing the risk of fungal attacks, especially in the autumn.

In colder climates, the angle and direction of early morning sun in winter should also be studied. Frost may otherwise persist too long into the day. If there is drip from branches overhanging the green, they are too close in any case, but grass does not thrive in shade any more than it appreciates invasion by tree roots. Mole ploughing round the green or trenching and painting the severed roots with hormone weedkiller will be needed. Sometimes the future spread of the crown of the tree is forgotten when planting close to greens and tees. If there is any doubt, plant further out. This is particularly true in warmer climates where eucalyptus and wattle are quick growing, greedy of water and almost a weed.

These factors apply, in fact, more frequently to tees, as we have seen, because it is relatively simple to put a tee back into woodland without disturbing the general effect, but a narrow gap leads to excessive shade and dampness.

The choice of trees for new planting on a golf course should be related to the landscape generally, but it is just as important to plant in keeping with the artificial landscape which the golf course itself creates over its hundred acres or so. By the sea, on sandy or gravelly heaths, and in pine woods, the answer is ready made. Elsewhere, the importation of sand and the slow development of an acid turf should temper the selection. Initially, a basis of pine and silver birch is widely adaptable and fills the gap until hardwoods can develop. Pines provide greenery throughout the year while the deciduous birch has small leaves which blow away easily. It is a very agreeable mixture in itself with the white trunks amongst dark green tufts of needles. The planting plan should provide for varying and contrasting densities and never be set out on a precise 50:50 basis. Other conifers can be added sparingly to vary colour and form but those with formal habits of growth should seldom be used in isolation. Some of these are also tempting for young neighbours at Christmas. Similarly, most cyprus and thuya look better in the garden than on the golf course.

Birch may not last much more than one generation. Specimens planted at Addington Court, Surrey in 1910 were still growing in 1980 but tending to die off and suffer fungal attacks. There was no natural regeneration due to play and upkeep operations on a tightly planned layout.

Fig. 4.26 The rolling country round Auchterarder lent itself well to translating seaside classicism into the more romantic conception of Gleneagles, no. 14. (H.W. Neale, Action Photos.)

Oak, beech, single specimens of mountain ash, the wild cherry (gean) can be added, preferably away from greens, but chestnuts, planes, maples (except the hedge maple), sycamore, ash and limes give leaf problems and may have the wrong associations. They will, therefore, be better sited away from greens, tees, and bunkers and probably as single specimens or groups of three. Bunkers especially should be avoided because they are often designed to avoid sand blowing and are correspondingly more likely to retain a deep carpet of dead leaves. Poplars are generally best avoided unless landscaping a stream or pool, but local considerations rule near water as they do in parkland courses where noble specimens may need replacing. On boundaries they can be quick and effective, but other types in front of them will improve appearance. Weeping and 'blue' forms of otherwise acceptable species should also be treated with reserve.

The line between what is wrong on a golf course and right in a garden gets more difficult to draw when choosing shrubs. Gorse and broom obviously qualify for the golfing landscape: sallow and spindle also grow wild and there are plenty of colourful hawthorns. Rhododendrons may be more demanding but there are heathers which tolerate lime. The less vivid azaleas, forsythia and dogwoods (but not variegated) might be adopted, but one should stop short of berberis, double-flowered almonds and other common delights of the smaller garden.

Exotic subjects can be planted between the club house and the first tee, but from that point on, the landscape should be native or at least naturalized while accepting imports with informal associations and tolerant of possible exposure. To go beyond these fairly elementary guide lines, consultations with landscape architects are indicated.

The birch + pine mixture is about the only one which can be recommended generally for golf course use, but it barely touches the fringe of all the possibilities. Existing trees will obviously affect choice and soil types cannot be ignored. Therefore, it may be more useful to list a few principles:

1. *Unity* This factor should relate not only to the types planted, but their relation to the form of the site. Tree planting should move with the contours and horizons. Plant groups, not lines; clumps, not avenues.

2. *Graduation* Link major tree groups to open space with diminishing groups and specimens.

Soften hard edges with lower growing trees or shrubs. Let salients and re-entrants break any suggestion of a sharp outline along fairways. Plan glades to lighten dark areas.

3.   *Contrast* Opposition of form and colour can create striking effects. Contrast trees with an open head against those with denser foliage. Avoid simple mixtures of deciduous types.

4.   *Harmony* On wooded sites, respect established patterns and types. Compatible planting, however, need not slavishly follow surrounding species. The golf course is big enough to be treated as a landscape unit in its own right.

Many of these rules in reverse should guide clearing wooded sites. Leave specimen trees, leave space for air to circulate, leave a broken outline. Consider what vista may be opened up by clearing a fairway.

Remember that trees that have been growing densely in a wood will not appear very elegant when their bare sides are revealed. They may also be subject to wind-blow.

Limit clearing of undergrowth to the essential margins because it may be restricting surface run-off from slopes and be preventing erosion. It also has ecological importance.

Planting on a grand scale with pine, juniper, beech and other hard woods, still gives the Goodwood Golf Course and its surroundings a unique character some 200 years later.

And while on the South Coast, inspect the 'hollow' rings of conifers and birch planted in the early thirties on the lower levels of the Hill Barn golf course at Worthing by my father (Fig. 4.27).

Some clubs have dedicated remote areas and planted forest nursery stock costing a few pounds per thousand. Planting is rapid being a dibbing rather than a digging operation, but losses are severe because planting in grass is not the same as replanting cleared woodland where vegetation is sparser and brambles give protection. Many trees have a system of fine root hairs, hardly noticed when they are pulled up. These are busy in just the same area as grass roots. The 2×1 transplant stands a poor chance against hefty clumps of cocksfoot. After a few years, unless clearing round each tree has been regular, it is difficult to see either the wood or the trees. Near play, the upkeep of the rough normally demands a minimum planting interval of triple gang mower width or, better

Fig. 4.27   The 8th at Hill Barn, among the South Downs behind Worthing. The plantation beyond the line of earlier pines is a big hollow circle, but being mostly evergreens looks solid throughout the year. Planted in the early 1930s. (H.W. Neale, Action Photos.)

still, 5 metres. Very small trees would not stand much chance if the spacing is minimal. Planting cheaper whips may exaggerate this difficulty if they are near play.

'Instant' trees have become more interesting as more specially prepared stock has become available. Unless so prepared they must be transplanted by the machines designed for the job. But it is still desirable to prepare larger trees on the course to be transplanted by trenching round and filling the trench with peat a year or two before they are moved. And it still has to be demonstrated that 25 ft of lanky tree, which may need guy ropes for a year or two is better than a tall standard which will develop into a handsome shape and be a feature in under ten years if properly planted.

Container grown trees can be planted over an extended season whereas those lifted from open ground should only be moved between October and March. But larger trees may still be best transplanted gently, quickly and moistly. If an interval between arrival and planting is inevitable ensure that they are heeled into damp soil.

Parkland courses and many inland sites have a legacy of past planting to be preserved. Total reliance on the survival of mature specimens often leads to a crash programme contrived too late when age, storm and disease take a severe toll over a wide area. Part of the greenkeeper's task should be an annual review of important trees. This can be quite simple but keeps the whole question under review. Replacements can then be planted in good time, spacing them according to eventual size from 5 metres up to 15 metres for big trees.

Repair of damage, especially broken branches, is sometimes left too long until rot has started. Sometimes the remnants of the branch are sawn off a foot or so from the trunk which invites further rotting. The cut should be made close to the trunk where it will callous over. Young trees and bushes should be brushed up from time to time to encourage shapely growth and also to facilitate the search for lost balls amongst them. Where fairways are close, there is an awkward stage between planting and the formation of a canopy when grass still has to be cut frequently. Later, shade will change the dominant species and groundwork will lessen, though cleaning up may still be desirable from time to time. The large machines which gather and mulch leaves may be economic in densely afforested layouts and the recycling of well-rotted leaves in compost is clearly desirable and good house-keeping.

There are two 'gimmicks' in tree planting which ought to be treated with extreme caution. One is the practice of planting a single specimen of a particular species, generally an unusual one, at a set distance from greens, generally 150 yards. This action is not favoured in strategic planning. The other is to imitate the Augusta National course at Atlanta, Georgia where holes are planted with and named after a particular shrub. One may assume that in that case the objective, which is not normal in landscaping on a big scale has been achieved with skill though the list of varieties is often exotic. The rest of us would probably be well advised not to try it at Sludgecombe-on-Ouse. In any case the Augusta site was part nursery before it was a golf course.

Sea buckthorn provides one example of how the excessive encouragement of local species or importing species from similar situations can go awry. A Burnham member is said to have brought in a few plants to Burnham and Berrow in the early days. It took over large stretches of rough, and creeps inexorably inland as birds drop the seeds from its orange berries, after feasting on them in late summer when the ripe fruit smells like the vendange in Burgundy. It also affords an impenetrable protective cover for rabbits and is difficult, uncomfortable and expensive to remove.

Tree planting can still improve a golf course when all else has been done. Many Committees discuss it – not so many carry it through to its logical conclusion. A good example of what can be done on a standard inland course, both from the landscape and playing points of view, can be seen at the South Staffordshire Golf Club at Tettenhall. Further north, the club enjoying the excellent H.S. Colt layout at Prestbury in Cheshire has, over the past few years, completed a well planned and implemented programme of tree-planting. All the old virtues of the course remain and a new dimension has been given to a group of holes like 1, 6, 9 and 18.

Two very good examples of what can be done by thoughtfully placed and well chosen trees in warmer climates can be seen at 'The Royal' and the Country Club, Johannesburg. J.R. (Roy) Anderson was guided by an unerring instinct for what is right. There are also many beautifully, if more exotically, planted courses in Sydney. Pennant Hills is one of the best and still presents a golfing landscape even though it is a lush one. These show that the oasis of scattered palm trees which seems to have bedevilled the planting of certain Spanish golf courses is neither rational nor necessary in hotter climates. It does however seem to suit Marrakech which *is* an oasis.

Occasionally trees can be used on either side of the entrance to a green though for practical reasons discussed, not too close to it. While perfectly legitimate where the trees are, so to speak, discovered during the preparation of the layout, this is hardly a device which can be introduced using imported native trees. Damage can be severe and if the trees die the strategy has to be re-thought. A better effect is obtained by one tree judiciously placed to guard one side of the green. This can replace and be stronger than a bunker especially when promoting the advantage of a particular line of play at a dog-legged hole as suggested earlier.

All the trouble taken in selecting and planning will be set at naught if the planting is not done with all the care lavished on a putting green. And care must continue afterwards. Thorough preparation of the holes with more than the maximum diameter, careful spreading of the roots, not planting too deeply, fine soil enriched with compost and some bonemeal, well firmed round them but not puddled, a stout stake for the first few years, a flexible but firm tie, physical protection (especially, where necessary, wire netting part sunk into the ground to deter rabbits) – nothing can be neglected. Protecting the lower trunk from rabbits, hares and vermin is equally essential. If planting is done at the right season, only an exceptional drought need cause alarm and there is nothing against judicious fertilizing with or without water. Then if the grass is kept back (and contact herbicides sprayed with a shield simplify this), if tree-ties are checked, vermin kept out and errant golfers exhorted, it is surprising how soon a plantation will begin to make a show. Life is not so short on a golf course and future generations will be grateful for what is done now, even if it is only to start a nursery to make the job cheaper in their time.

4.6 WATER

The limitations of the golf course architect's vocabulary have already been mentioned. The 'proper' architect has a variety of materials, forms, colours, textures and styles and when these are exhausted, can still pursue originality and invention into the surroundings of his building. The golf course architect has only turf, sand and water as basic materials, with contour and trees in the third

Fig. 4.28 The par 3, no. 17 at Mortonhall, Edinburgh, uses water, rock, whins, rushes and trees to feature a 'highland' setting some five miles from Princes Street. (Courtesy of S.R. Jamieson, Edinburgh.)

dimension. These limitations have reacted in favour of water. It was little used in the past unless it happened to be on the site already. Today it can be used on a big scale with dramatic and lovely effects which take the mind back to the great days of landscaping and to masterly realizations like Blenheim at Woodstock.

It must be said that satiation as well as saturation may occur where, as was recently reported of a new hyper-layout, water comes into play at 17 holes. This is clearly only for the champions. For the rest of us, water is so final a hazard that its constant repetition in play soon palls. Whereas the courage and concentration can be wound up once or twice in 18 holes to meet the challenge of water, to wind them up on 17 or possibly more occasions very soon exhausts the glands supplying the necessary tonic substances to the blood stream and the handicap player will tack listlessly round the obstacles and may even forget to appreciate their visual charm.

Another of those eclectic layouts of 18 of the greatest golf holes chosen by four very eminent golfers included just eight holes where water was operative – five inland and three seaside. That is certainly enough.

Landscaping with water features must form part of the original concept. It is rare to be able to construct anything bigger than a few hundred square yards in area on an existing course. The exceptions are generally links with a high water table. But oddly enough, the water feature often seems less appropriate on a links than inland and it can be a nuisance if it attracts small children as water inevitably seems to do.

If there is no water running through the feature, it is desirable that a minimum depth of $4\frac{1}{2}$ ft (1.35 m) should be provided. Shallow pools warm and green up in summer as algae multiply in the cosy environment. Evaporation will also be quicker and leave an unsightly margin to the water area unless it is topped up from the mains supply.

The margins will usually be graded gently to permit mowing down to the water's edge, if the feature is all in play. If part is left to naturalize, it is surprising how quickly flags and rushes appear and thrive. That is the next problem of upkeep if they start to march inexorably towards the middle. There are chemical and mechanical aids to resist choking up, but the former are not popular with environmentalists.

Fig. 4.29   Widening a stream to produce material for construction and a simple dam produced this water feature at the par 3, no. 16 at Downshire Golf Course, Easthampstead. (Courtesy of Chris Bakhurst.)

There are less problems with running water. The feature will then be created by widening and, if necessary, deepening, while damming up the downstream end. The meander of a stream also frequently follows a broader flat-bottomed valley which was the former river bed. Here simple damming may produce the feature desired. The River Board will generally need consultation and have wide powers which include control over new discharges of land drains. In flood plains, they can also control re-contouring.

Occasionally proposals are made for forming pools on sloping land. These should normally be resisted as any significant size will require massive banking at the lower end, even in quite gentle slopes. It should also be noted that a reservoir containing more than a certain gallonage must be executed, according to law, by a qualified engineer.

Every watery project, large or small, must respect visibility. The pleasures of seeing a golf ball fail to make the crossing and splash into the water might be debated. But no discussion is possible where not even the splash is seen, far less the water feature. This important factor must obviously be studied from the area whence the relevant shot will normally be played. In practice a profile of the complete hole should be prepared with the line of sight, green level, water level and all other relevant factors plotted on it. If the proposed lake is in a valley just short of the green and will not be seen from the earlier part of the fairway, the project is off unless the depth of the valley is such that the water level can be brought up into view.

Running streams have been part of the classic golfing scene since golf began. No. 11 at Merion, the short US championship course, provides a good example of how to profit from this hazard. This hole is not long – 370 yards at full stretch – but more length would be superflous. It is not perfect. The fairway drops after about 200 yards and the brow conceals the landing area and the stream crossing the fairway diagonally at about 280 yards. One would have liked to see the whole picture from the tee, but the days when complete holes were re-contoured were yet to come.

The rest of the hole is uniformly strong. The stream continues on and embraces the right side of the green. The putting area is elevated and only of average size. The fairway bunkering is not an intimate part of the strategic design built round the stream, but earns good marks for visual effect and putting some balancing interest into the earlier part of the hole. Quite a small sand bunker covers the left side of the entrance – simple, effective, a change of colour, and emphasizing the water on the right.

The stream crosses in front of the green at about a 45° angle, from left to right. This gives a splendid diagonal feeling to the hazard and leads up to the climax. If the second shot also has that 'going away' feeling, only doom can be expected. But that gives the heroic quality, which allied to strategic placing of the drive short of the stream and the penal fairway bunkering, makes the hole a text-book classic.

There is a lack of featuring beyond and indeed all round the green. There is no need to emphasize the drama of a green position with water down one side and the gentler marriage with the surrounding contours is subtle and correct.

Frequently, it will be necessary to divert a stream to provide drama of this sort but that can be much less complicated than might be thought. It will often be introduced to put the final touches to a situation where the *genius loci* just failed to put in the correct meander. And 'meander', of course, is just what any new water-course or even drainage ditch should do.

In countries in Africa where there is severe run-off and water is precious, the lake or dam is an essential part of the physical planning. The layout must be adapted to it and the land moulded to use it fully. In tropical latitudes, the life which swarms in or around the water is incredible and it will take regular attention to maintain a stable situation.

Even in temperate climes, the artificial water feature cannot be left to its own devices. Cleaning will be necessary from time to time. Recent research, fortunately, has much improved the prospects of removing unwanted growth without damage to fish and animal population. The Green Committee will be expected to know all about that as well.

5 Construction

'We but teach bloody instructions,
which, being taught, return to plague
the inventor.'

Shakespeare, *Macbeth*

5.1 METHOD

Once the master plan has been determined, detailed layouts and working drawings enable the full Specification and Bill of Quantities to be prepared. These are the essence of golf course construction. There are some who still think golf course architecture stops at the stage of a few loops on a plan indicating how eighteen holes might be arranged. But to enable a proper Specification and Bill of Quantities to be prepared, an accurate plan based on an equally accurate survey with contours at half metre or two foot intervals has to be produced and backed up by working drawings defining the form and levels of greens, tees and bunkers. The plan will be the whole basis for land drainage, earth movement and water system, even if local levels are still necessary for individual green designs. Indeed, on heavily wooded sites it is difficult for the golf course architect to move without a contoured plan prepared from an aerial survey.

There will be elements in the specification requiring specialist advice (e.g. soil amelioration, fertility levels, grass seed varieties). The determination of these matters is no longer done by eye or guess-work or by the feel of the soil between finger and thumb. The hydraulic conductivity of soil mixtures to be used will be determined in the laboratory. Samples must be taken and tested throughout the work. There are now highly qualified consultants in this field and they should be brought into the team at an early stage.

Fig. 5.1 The short 7th at Mortonhall is tucked into the scarps of the Braid Hills without undue artifice. (Courtesy of S.R. Jamieson, Edinburgh.)

With advice in those directions, the Bill of Quantities can be completed by the golf course architect so that comparative tenders can be obtained. It is unwise to embark on a golf course without the descriptions, calculations and safeguards which traditional methods of contracting procedure have built into the client/architect or engineer/contractor relationship. There is no mystery about making a golf course. It can be fully described in words and drawings. Unless that is done, the client cannot be sure of getting what he pays for. Similarly, the conditions of contract must be clearly defined and the standard document of the institution of Civil Engineers is more widely applicable than that of the R.I.B.A. I have been fortunate in having the help of A.H.F. Jiggens in setting up a documentation apt for golf-course contracts. He turned to golf course architecture from being City Engineer at Chester and has planned and designed golf courses in Ireland and Wales as well as northern England and the Midlands.

Tenders will normally be invited from a selected list rather than by public advertisement. One or two smaller local firms known to be reliable may be included as well as firms operating on a national basis.

Owing to the long gap between the last boom in golf course construction in the twenties, and the recent resurgence, even the biggest firms have not had all that long experience. A slapdash approach may derive from ignorance. The golf course architect must ensure that this does not continue.

The successful tender may still need adjustment to fit into the total estimate for the scheme. This is where the experienced golf architect can really prove his worth. The savings he makes will have been unjustified if some aspect of the job is eventually unsatisfactory but he must sometimes try to trim and vary the specification to produce acceptable results at a lower figure, even at some measure of risk of his own reputation. There is also scope for postponing some elements (e.g. less teeing ground or bunkers initially). But drainage and green specification should not be cut too fine.

The sudden expansion of golf course construction inspired many general contracting firms to enter the field and new companies to be set up. There is a general but misguided belief that the construction of a golf course is like building a sports ground with knobs on. Professional golfers have also teamed up with constructors to capitalize on names made known through tournament play.

Not all newcomers lack competence but the ability to take a scheme right through from initial planning into playing condition and ultimate success is only likely to develop after due apprenticeship and formal training in some subjects comprised in the total discipline.

The notion that playing skill alone is sufficient qualification for golf architecture has lost ground progressively since 1910 though there is obviously some sense in which it is important and coming back into vogue. The selection of a consultant, therefore, demands care, research, enquiry and comparison. Even the opinion of an earlier promoter should be treated with reserve because of the human tendency to inflate the merits of personal ventures. Inspect and judge with help from neutral observers if needed.

At the same time, the connection of a well-known player's name with a new course will help publicity and may attract more green fees. Resort golf courses and hotels still sponsor better known players as 'Golf Director' or as 'Tournament Professional'.

The twenties have also returned to the scene with a number of 'package-deal' (design and construct) firms with or without an attached professional golfer. Quite frequently, two professionals pair up for mutual support. Obviously the same caution is advisable in selection but some additional pitfalls are present. The connection of layout and design with expenditure involves the danger that the extent or quality of the work will be adjusted towards maximum profit or avoidance of loss. A Bill of Quantities and full Specification would help to reduce this danger but assume a third party to verify operations as work proceeds and to avoid disputes at the end. A fixed price is not compatible with operating on that basis. The client, therefore, risks paying for work not done or materials not supplied, thus shouldering and paying for risks normally undertaken by the contractor.

Whatever system is employed, the client should be ready to take over maintenance at the appropriate time. Early and regular mowing is the only road to goof turf. Leaving the grass for hay, or mowing it once a month, only produces a stubble and discourages the right grasses. Development on proper lines in the first year depends entirely on proper management. Whatever money has been spent on the project, once completed, it will go backwards at the critical time unless a skilled team looks after it from the time the contract stops to the day the first ball is played.

Irrespective of length or area, the ultimate in specifications should be recommended if wear on the course is expected to be heavy. A rise in standards has followed the rise in the number of golfers and accounts for some of the corresponding rise in construction costs. Amongst all the practical factors, drainage in one form or another is the one most likely to demand attention, not only because good drainage assists resistance to heavy use but also because it limits the time in which the course is out of play and, therefore unprofitable. It is equally essential for the health of grass which has to be irrigated artificially because of low rainfall. The proper selection and use of materials increase in importance each year. As I said earlier this is now a highly specialized field, and the one where the amateur can most quickly come to grief.

5.2   SPECIFICATION

The work necessary in making a new golf course must be fully described in the words of a Specification, the figures of Bills of Quantity and the Contract Drawings. No major project should be launched without these safeguards and they are equally useful on minor works. They assist in foreseeing the problems of carrying out the works as well as avoiding doubt and possible later dissension over the extent of the work to be undertaken by the parties concerned.

The specimen pages in Appendix 4 only give extracts, but they will enable a surveyor member to adapt his normal format to the lesser precision of making a green or a tee. The headings under which the work can be ranged in the specification are set out below. The Bills of Quantity then follow and will echo all the work described and preferably be numbered under a related system so that the contractor, when pricing each item, can readily refer to all the responsibilities his unit-rate has got to cover.

The Specification headings which should be considered are firstly the Contract Conditions, the general description of the work, the site, access, (very important on a golf course), contract period and maintenance period. All these are standard clauses in any engineering contract, but building a golf course needs similar controls.

Next come general responsibilities, definitions and administrative matters: Specification and Drawings; Bills of Quantities; Sanitary/Welfare Accommodation; Clerk of Works; Setting out Works; Workmanship; Hand Work; Machinery; Inclement Weather; Extra Works; Day Works; Routine Upkeep; Payments; Fluctuation of Prices.

The section on materials follows (quoting British Standards wherever possible), routine checks on quality and so on. Eleven headings generally suffice: Samples; Materials on Site; Delivery; Sand; Peat; Topsoil; Site Soil; Aggregate; Drain Pipes; Chemicals; Grass Seed.

Now we can get down to work, starting with site clearance: Herbage; Trees; Bushes and Shrubs; Derelict Buildings; Fences; Rubbish, Loose Stones and Boulders.

Next, following so far as possible the pattern which the work will follow, we deal with earth movement with descriptions of the sort of formation which will be demanded by the drawings. This part of the operation can be covered under: Topsoil Removal; Subsoil Grading; Greens, Approaches, Surrounds; Tees; Bunkers; Fairways and Rough; Pools; Rates for Fill; Respreading Topsoil.

The very important drainage section has to be detailed almost down to the sea. This is work too easily scamped by taking old-fashioned short cuts which, time has shown, lead to early problems. There are nineteen sections in order to cover all parts of the work: Topsoil Excavation; Subsoil Excavation; Laying; Junctions; Filling; Topsoil replacement; Catchwater Drains; Drainage Layer; Silt Pits, Inspection Chambers; Outlets; Soakaways; Mole Drainage; Ditch Cleaning; Ditch Piping; Drain Lay; New Ditches; Culverts; Subsoil Cultivation.

Having built, drained, and respread topsoil, we can next get down to preparation and sowing. The first section will be subdivided into greens, tees and approaches: Ploughing; Cultivation; Soil Amelioration – Putting Areas, Teeing Areas, and Approaches; Hand Raking and Heeling; Fertilizer Treatment; Stone Removal; Sowing; Turf; Turf Laying.

Then come fairways and rough: Ploughing; Cultivating; Blade Grading; Ground Limestone (Provisional); Soil Amelioration; Seed Bed Preparation; Fertilizer Treatment; Stone Removal; Sowing; Stone Removal; Rolling; Mowing. (*N.B.* Stone removal needs very careful definition.)

Sometimes it is practical to retain grass already growing on the site if the area is big enough, the quality good enough, and the surface smooth enough. Six headings cover this work: Harrowing; Rolling; Mowing; Fertilizer Treatment; Lime Treatment; Weed Killing.

Tree Planting gets a section to itself, being specialized work: B.S. 3936; Half Standard; Standard; Feathered Tree; Conifer; Season; Tree Pits; Backfill; Staking; Planting; Tying; Tree Guards; Spacing; Guarantee.

Finally, the contractor's duties under maintenance have to be specified. Number of cuts, at what height, and all the operations which may be necessary. The first heading has to be very carefully worded. The rest are straightforward green-keeping: Responsibilities; Greens and Tees; Hand Rolling; Mowing; Renovation; Weeds; Fairways and Rough; Watering; Completion; Bunker Cleaning and Sand Spreading.

The development of some of these headings can be seen in the typical Specification pages in Appendix 4. I have selected some which are normally of prime importance.

5.3   BILLS OF QUANTITY

These are normally best presented in eight sections as follows:

Bill no. 1 *Preliminaries*
Provides for the contractor to allow for responsibilities imposed by the contract conditions and specification such as Site Office, setting-out, soil sampling.

Bill no. 2 *Site Clearance*
Removal of fences, hedges, debris, herbage, bushes, trees, stumps, derelict buildings and cleaning streams or pools. Lengths and types of fence, and disposal. Girth of trees will be described in detail with areas and numbers provided.

Bill no. 3 *Earth Movement*
This Bill will cover borrow pits, transport of material, formation of greens, tees and bunkers. Green

construction should be itemized individually with volumes concerned, e.g. 'Green no. 15. Cut; 200 m³. Fill; 850 m³'. The formation of any pools, adjustment of fairway contours and respreading topsoil will also be covered here.

Bill no. 4 *Installation of Water System*
This is conveniently done at this time or just after.

Bill no. 5 *Drainage*
Showing lengths of all drains, dimensions, ditch cleaning, junctions, French drains, chambers, headwalls, weirs and sometimes mole ploughing.

Bill no. 6 *Preparation and Sowing*
Supply of sand, peat, topsoil, herbicide, fertilizer, grass seed, limestone, followed by the operations required and their areas. Greens, Tees, Fairways and Rough will form three sections and there is often a fourth for existing grassland to be retained.

Bill no. 7 *Tree Planting*
Types, number, size, varieties.

Bill no. 8 *Maintenance*
Here will be charged the number of cuts which the contractor is to carry out after germination, the operations to be performed before handing over, supply of bunker sand and spreading.

Specimen Bill of Quantity pages are set out in Appendix 4. Probably the most difficult calculation is the volume of soil to be moved from an irregular area to form an even more irregularly shaped green. It is a long tedious process but the only fair way for the golf course architect to do his job and to provide a reasonably sound estimate of costs in the early stages.

5.4   DRAWINGS

The following schedule of drawings accompanied documents and invitations to tender for a municipal golf course in Kent in 1981.

		Scale	*Contours*
1.	General layout	1/1250	1 m intervals
2.	Drainage	1/1250	1 m intervals
3.	Site clearance/ditch cleaning	1/1250	1 m intervals
4.	Main borrow areas/cultivation treatment	1/1250	1 m intervals
5.	18 green plans	1/200	0.25 m intervals
6.	18 tee plans	1/200	0.25 m intervals
7.	(a) Detailed layout pool areas	1/500	———
	(b) Longitudinal sections	1/500	1/100 vertical scale
	(c) Cross-sections and weir details	1/500	1/100 vertical scale
	(details	1/20)	

These drawings enable a contractor to estimate from a clear knowledge of the golf course architect's requirements and later to carry out the works accurately and in a logical order.

The same skeleton site plan serves as the basis for Plans 1 to 4. The remainder are based on local surveys. It is desirable to relate green levels to the same datum as the general plan.

A layout plan with a few loops and doodles all over it and green plans which show so-called levels (+3, +8, +12 in) unrelated to existing ground levels and even to each other are no longer adequate. With golf courses costing from a quarter to a half a million pounds, it is only fair to the client and the contractor that the preparatory work should be impeccable. That is only possible where each green and tee site is surveyed, a level grid prepared, and the drawings show the designs for the whole of the greens and tees in new contours. A contoured aerial survey will generally suffice as a basis for general drainage plans and profiles along lines of play. The cost of this is small in the total budget, but invaluable throughout the job. If green plans are drawn intelligently and interpreted precisely, any subsequent modification will be very small and easily achieved. It will be no more than the varnishing stage of the oil painting. A slight retouch is permissible here and there because, being three dimensional, the relation of the new form to horizon cannot accurately be visualized beforehand. It will normally relate to moulding the surface, which may be so subtle that normal contour intervals cannot intelligibly describe it.

5.5   CLERK OF WORKS

Although the size of the job and its pace may not justify a full time Clerk of Works, it is highly desirable that a competent supervisor visit the site daily and occupy say four hours a day, not always the same ones, verifying the contractor's operations especially during drainage and water installation and the spreading of stone and topsoil mix on the greens. The first two of these operations are going to be covered up so it is important to check grades, junctions, line and depth before the pipes are hidden. The last two are more easily verified from the surface but even so it is a great nuisance if there are found to be deficiencies.

The Clerk of Works will also act as a general controller of day to day operations and decide if weather conditions dictate a halt.

On new municipal courses, a Clerk of Works can generally be provided from the Technical Services Department. On private jobs the head greenkeeper will generally be appointed at an early date so that he will be familiar with all subterranean services provided. However, many greenkeepers are strong in maintenance and relatively inexperienced in constructional techniques, as one would expect, so some additional control is desirable by the golf course architect's organization.

Most firms operate conscientiously but any less trustworthy must be controlled in this way. It is not so much the desire to deceive that is the danger as the belief that the grass will still grow even if the site has been panned down for months by big machinery. The Clerk of Works has to ensure that the soil remains in good shape mechanically from the surface down into the subsoil so that the young grass roots will go down deeply in the early days of establishment. The tines on the back of a bulldozer will not ensure this but a subsoil cultivator pulled through at the right depth and interval will repair much damage to the soil structure. Another implement which needs strict control is the rotary cultivator. It is all too easy for a blithe operator to fluff up cart tracks and conceal conditions below, which will produce a stodgy surface with a sickly crop of grass for years to come.

The weekly or biweekly visits of the golf course architect at critical times will avoid most of these errors but for steady progress and to avoid going back over past history, the day to day control by the Clerk of Works helps client, architect and, indeed, the Contractor.

There is apparently a belief in some quarters that if a change is made in formations completed by the contractor, this will cost the client more money. Such a belief can only arise from a total ignorance of the whole procedure recommended here or from an obstinate belief in the virtue of others.

If the contractor does not produce the correct formation according to the plan provided, he is obliged to correct it at his own expense. This responsibility has the happy effect of inclining him to get it right first time. The Clerk of Works will help him to avoid the need to go back by pointing out discrepancies, if they occur, when they occur.

6 Practical politics

'It is quite certain that, had the
ground on which ordinary inland golf
is played today been the only available
ground for the purpose, the game
would never have been invented at all
. . . .'

Garden G. Smith, *The World of Golf* (1898)

6.1 THE HEAD GREENKEEPER

It is not uncommon to hear employers of labour complain about the frequent turnover of staff. If that creates difficulties we can imagine how much worse it would be for the staff if the managing director changed every two or three years. This is what happens to greenkeepers and is probably the worst element in their task. They establish a happy fruitful relationship with one Green Convener then suddenly he is called off and a substitute sent on. Human nature being rather more difficult to change than the pH of a fairway, there will inevitably be times when relations are less harmonious than they should be. The wife of one American golf course superintendent (as they were called in the USA before moving up to course manager) once wrote that she knew when the Greens [sic] Chairman was a bad one. It reacted throughout her home life. For a highly trained specialist, ill-considered interference can be an anathema.

It is important that the new chairman should know something of the background of his new team. Greenkeepers are excellent citizens and addicted to the philosophy of self-help. For 70 years they have helped themselves and their knowledge by lectures, discussions, educational visits and their monthly magazine. They also started an apprenticeship scheme, which they ran themselves for ten years before the Golf Development Council took it over and renamed it the Greenkeeper Training Committee. In that period they produced over 200 basically trained recruits to greenkeeping while golf itself did nothing. They did all this out of their own time and limited resources. They initiated a Turf Grass Symposium for general education which has continued at regular intervals ever since. Golf itself has organized very few open meetings and those have been about the rules and general matters. The golf trade, however, organized the Golf Foundation, which has done nothing but good. The rest of the big money in golf has gone to the Open Championship, the Overseas Touring Fund, cigarette publicity, the Professional Golfer's Association, and some management teams. All this has put golf on the map, but not the greenkeepers. Golf itself invests little in training, research, development and labour relations. Responsibility is dispersed among a Rules body, four ethnic groups, a joint committee called CONGU and a number of self-interested associations. Every organization is represented on every other one to provide a sense of cohesion and efficiency, but from the business angle there is effective stalemate outside each organization's immediate concern.

Even now, there is still no effective recruitment into greenkeeping. Older courses can just find them. New ones have to take pot luck. The average age of ground staff in Great Britain has, at a guess, gone down from 40 to 20 in fifteen years. Traditional greenkeeping practices are in danger of being lost because we have all been too slow in realizing the side effects of developing golf alone and not its associated trades.

The new Green Convener can repair many of these omissions at local level if he is so minded. He should encourage all his staff to belong to British, Scottish, or European Golf Greenkeepers Association, or their equivalents in the USA, Australia and New Zealand, even if the club pays the subscriptions. He should encourage their attendance at lectures, factory visits (for example to Ransomes at Ipswich or Sisis at Macclesfield) and the Association's annual meeting. He should see that all attend one of the 5-day courses run in Spring and Autumn at the Sports Turf Research

Institute or at various centres in Europe by the international organization, and a visit to the GCSAA annual conference and show at the start of the year will be a revelation and an inspiration. He should ensure that all get the opportunity to play golf and that they get tuition from the club professional. This part of his job will alone produce big dividends in the standard of upkeep.

The head greenkeeper will naturally settle his own salary and conditions at the time of joining the club and will make wage or other representations on behalf of his staff as necessary. His Chairman will be the most effective instrument in ensuring a contented work-force. But there will be much more to the relationship than that.

The head greenkeeper should produce a monthly report which can be circulated to the Green Committee a few days before their regular meetings. The greenkeeper should attend these meetings, go through the report, and be prepared to answer questions. In this way, he can be sure that the more superficial comments of members generally can be put into perspective at source.

The competition programme will be discussed at the beginning of the year and the winter programme of course repairs and improvements in late summer, though plans for any major works should have been discussed and finalized in the Spring.

Once a year he will prepare his budget and list the machinery and materials which he wishes to be purchased. Before doing this, he will have prepared a schedule of all his machinery noting age, condition, petrol consumption and usefulness, with recommendations for sale, repair, exchange, replacement or scrap.

He should have authority for discreet, on the spot reproval of members whose actions on the course fall short of a certain standard. In this respect, like the club professional, he is the custodian of a great deal of golfing lore and etiquette which have come down to him in his training. Perhaps because they have their feet literally on the ground, greenkeepers have retained much more of the respect for it which older golfers seemed to experience.

This aspect of his duties will be simplified if he keeps members informed via the club noticeboard of all impending operations likely to interfere with play. At the same time he can politely draw attention to damage which might be avoidable, young trees needing care, trolley routes needing to be changed, machinery damage which has occurred because of litter. If he is given his own corner of the noticeboard, he can also pin up from time to time those articles concerning frost greens, winter tee mats and the like, which he thinks would be helpful to members' understanding of his and the course's problems.

He will, however, be responsible to one person only – his Chairman. No other member of the club may make direct complaints or suggestions to him, apart from those frivolous remarks at which, if he is not too old, he may manage a weary smile.

The greenkeeper, after all, may have charge of an investment worth half a million pounds which is subject to the vagaries of weather and golfers. He must evaluate recommendations ranging from the latest abstract research to the *ad hoc* suggestions of representatives of fertilizer firms with an axe to grind. He has to assess the long-term effect of immediate benefits and the immediate effect of obtaining long-term benefits. It is not a simple job, but with help from the Green Convener, it can be very rewarding.

6.2   ETIQUETTE

The enforcement of the code of behaviour which experience has shown to be necessary on a golf course devolves in many respects on those in charge of the course itself. The head greenkeeper will deal with infractions which he observes but he has a big area to cover. A constant underground campaign needs to be conducted in the club house to ensure that standards do not slip. Divots, pitch marks, bunkers are only the beginning.

The problem can be attacked on four fronts – danger, damage, delay, disturbance. All etiquette can be related to the need to avoid the four Ds and players should be encouraged on the following lines:

Danger

- Wait to play until the match ahead is out of range.

- Ensure that no one is in range of your club (practice swings as well) or standing dangerously close to your line.
- Give immediate 'Fore' warning if your ball heads unexpectedly for other players.
- Better to wait still longer for persons on nearby footpaths to move out of reach. They may not understand 'Fore!', nor how to protect themselves; and there may be children running round, though never, one hopes, on the golf course itself.
- Do not use clubs with loose heads or damaged shafts.
- Do not yield to the desire to throw the ball, a club or the whole bag into the trees, lake, etc.

Damage

- Replace divots. It is well known that crows and rooks remove them and that some disintegrate, but put them back just the same and press them down. Smooth out marks in the bunkers *after* you have made them.
- Prise up and press level pitch marks in greens. Do not practice swings on a tee.
- Leave trollies well away from greens and aprons. Do not lay golf bags on the putting surface. If necessary, lay the flag stick down but gently.
- Do not cross your feet and then lean on your putter.
- Keep feet as far as possible from the hole when retrieving a ball.
- Observe any local rules about dropping away from new trees.
- Observe notices forbidding trollies or indicating routes between holes or round obstacles.
- Observe rules giving relief from divot marks, *if any*.
- Observe winter rules for rolling a ball on fairways, *if any*.
- Consider 'multiple ball retrieval' in winter, i.e. one player collects all holed balls when putting is completed.

Delay

- Play promptly once it is safe to do so.
- Play a provisional ball if you doubt finding the first.
- Observe the five minute rule looking for a lost ball, but give up sooner if there is no hope.
- Call following players through:

1. If the full 5 minutes looks like being necessary.
2. If you have lost a clear hole on the match in front.
3. If there is space in front and you are obviously slower than those behind.
4. If requested as a matter of valid urgency, e.g. rendezvous with wife.

- Make your mind up about your next shot as far as possible before you reach the ball.
- Observe local priorities, e.g. starting tees for 2 and 4 ball matches.
- Never cut in without total assurance that you will not impede the progress of others. But allow others to cut in in front of you if you will not be much inconvenienced. They may be in a hurry or weary.
- Always watch the flight of your opponent's or partner's ball as well as your own and 'mark' its landing place.
- If your opponent wishes to walk in after a match accompany him, even if you are having the best round of your life.
- After putting out, leave the green at once. Mark cards on the next tee, where you may in any case have to wait a few moments.
- Mark balls on greens as sparingly as possible. Pick up immediately, if a putt is conceded in match play. In a 4-ball, pick up at once if your score is of no value.
- Do not be reluctant to strike first from tee no. 1. If handicaps are the same, toss a coin and get moving.

Disturbance

(a) Practical
- Don't bang your car door in the car-park. You may disturb someone on the first tee in the day time or someone asleep at night.
- Avoid all distracting activities near the first tee – talk, practice swings and movement.
- Stand still and quiet opposite the player never behind him or in line of his putt (or on it!). Keep your shadow out of his view when he is playing.
- Do not start to move off when you have played if your opponent (or partner) still has not done so.

(b) Psychological
- You may ask an opponent what his score is, but not tell him.
- Only say 'Good putt' after the ball has actually dropped, if it looks like an easy one. Be consistent in the concession (or otherwise) of putts.

6.3   SAFETY

The Green Convener may have to respond to a situation where golf balls are being frequently struck into the gardens of a house or into a road. His own members accept a certain risk when they step on to the golf course and internal accidents are more open to discussion. But there is no discussion possible about the duty of a golf club not to cause annoyance and danger to its neighbours. Even if the golf club has been in existence for a hundred years and the house for only one, the club must still take steps to avoid danger repeatedly occurring. Wherever possible the situation should be tackled earlier at the planning stage where marginal development is known to be in train. The expense and disturbance to which a golf club may be put if houses are built at a certain distance from certain points in fairways, may influence approval by the authority and produce a compromise solution. But building land being an expensive commodity and the fact that the public may still have access to the risk area in some other way may still oblige the club to consider its remedies.

The first reaction is frequently to build a tall wire fence. (This in itself may require planning permission.) The cases in which this is effective are relatively few. A well sliced or hooked golf ball is not thereby prevented from soaring to a considerable height. Maintenance of such screens is also a costly business over the years and if they are not properly maintained they are still more unsightly. They may be useful near tees in enforcing a certain line but the sort of player likely to require this enforcement is also the one likely to top the ball forward of the tee, whence his second shot can pursue the dangerous line unhindered. They also appear occasionally near tees inside the golf course where normal limits have not been observed. The situation must not be allowed to develop to the point where the aggrieved householder applies for an injunction to prevent the golf course using that particular hole until it is altered. If granted, this can reduce the course to 17 holes and to a temporary par 3 followed by a walk past the danger point. The maintenance of contact with the other party should be ensured from the time of his complaint until a solution is found. That solution on a well developed course nearly always seems to lead to some loss of length. If there is no spare land elsewhere that has to be accepted. It probably means that rather more length was provided previously than the area justified. So it will only be a question of putting the clock back.

6.4 FURNITURE

The most useful gift a golf club member can make to the club in his memory is a seat of teak or similar hardwood, not a silver trophy. Play is slower, congestion is greater and there is need for something to sit on at each tee. Even the small tree trunk set across two supporting stumps will serve but, like other fixed obstructions, leads to wear and sometimes mowing problems round it.

This heading extends much wider than seats to include shelters, signs, flags, tee markers and even the signs round the club house. But all these, except purpose-built shelters, can be studied in the appropriate trade catalogues. The intention here is rather to emphasize the problem of upkeep and to suggest that the choice of what is rugged and rustic rather than slick and colourful will weather better and stay respectable longer. Even then, some regular maintenance will postpone the onset of old age, with flaking paint, splitting grain, and other maladies which eventually afflict us all. If these appearances mar the impression of the first tee, something has already been lost.

Too many committee discussions end with the solution: 'Put up a notice!' Over the years a series of instructions appear, many no longer enforced and some superfluous as time goes by. Notices, direction signs and arrows should be limited to the bare essentials and wherever possible other ways of instructing and guiding players should be found. However, there should be no economy in providing signposts to guide visitors to the gates.

At La Baule, the visitor is picked up by a sign-post on the seafront and conducted three miles inland to the golf course. Formby and West Lancashire are two other well sign-posted golf courses. Unfortunately, Planning Officers are often obstructive to golf course signposts.

The other horn of this dilemma is the irritation to visitors if they are unable to locate following tees or, at worst, the appropriate green. The Royal Salisbury Golf Club in Zimbabwe maintains two sets of greens – winter and summer alternatives and both are fully designed. The result tends to be confusing to the eye. Even at home, situations arise where one flag can be mistaken for another. This is more likely at holes with the minimum of rough or, as at Auckland in New Zealand, none. There, only the trees hint at the composition of the hole as a unit.

Shelters round the course, preferably at strategic points serving several holes, are welcome and can be agreeable in themselves. Overlapping elm boards with cedar shingles last tolerably well and need minimum upkeep. Shelters should have a bench all round, be generally open and divided by three or four partitions to leave always one section unaffected by driving rain.

Visibility problems from tees have been overcome or reduced by a short flight of steps ending in space or a periscope and although it goes against the book, there is a simple pleasure in ringing the bell by the blind green to indicate to following players that they can play their approach shots.

Much doubt and many notices can be avoided if the score card has a clear simple plan of the layout and better still like Mount Mitchell Lands in North Carolina, a little thumb-nail sketch of each hole above its number (Fig. 6.1). Indeed the score-card goes straight to the heart of the

Mount Mitchell Golf Club
16 miles S.E. of Burnsville
on N.C. Highway 80
2 miles W. of Buck Creek Gap
exit of Blue Ridge Parkway
Sales Office · 675-4923
Pro Shop · 675-5454

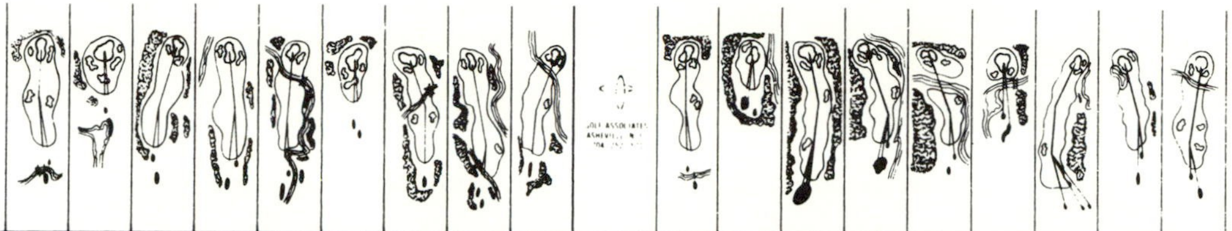

LOCAL RULES
U.S.G.A. Rules Govern Play · Register in Pro Shop before playing · O.B. white stakes · Free drop from sprinkler heads · Creeks & drainage ditches constitute water hazard · Keep carts away from tees, greens & traps · Repair ball marks & rake traps · Foursomes have priority · Allow faster players thru · Shirts must always be worn.

Hole	1	2	3	4	5	6	7	8	9	OUT	10	11	12	13	14	15	16	17	18	IN	TOT	HDP	NET	DATE
Blue Tees	330	200	370	380	520	170	340	500	360	3170	340	125	530	430	450	180	490	360	400	3305	6475			
+ or −																								
Par	4	3	4	4	5	3	4	5	4	36	4	3	5	4	4	3	5	4	4	36	72			
Handicap	18	6	12	11	5	14	9	13	10		8	16	3	2	1	4	15	17	7					
+ or −																								
White Tees	320	180	360	370	490	145	320	480	350	3015	330	110	490	410	420	160	480	350	390	3140	6155			
Red Tees	280	160	340	350	460	135	300	450	320	2795	290	100	430	370	350	110	430	320	330	2730	5525			

SCORER:
ATTEST:

Fig. 6.1   Plans of each hole assist planning, play and subsequent recollection. The water is less obvious than it looks. (Courtesy of Mount Mitchell Golf Course, North Carolina.)

problem if it is well designed. The Green Convener can land most of his messages precisely on target where they will count most. Since he will always carry one in his pocket while he is in office, he will have plenty of opportunities to reflect on ways in which the score card could be improved.

6.5 PRESENTATION

In 1775, the first rule of the Honourable Company of Edinburgh Golfers read:

'You must tee your Ball not nearer the Hole than two club lengths nor further distant from it than four'.

In 1832, the R. & A. decided to make two holes in each green, one for playing out and one for coming home.

In 1864, Royal North Devon's Rules required the ball to be teed not nearer the hole than six club lengths and not further from it than eight.

So, even the earliest green committees started to ease playing conditions as time went on. And by 1887, back in Scotland, the Golfing Annual entry for Luffness, as we saw earlier, said:

> 'The putting greens on the whole are very fair, several of them having turf fit for a bowling green and almost dead level'.

So the idea of fair play on the greens came to the fore in a mere hundred years. In the next hundred it extended out to the rest of the course.

The philosophy behind this development is simple. If you play well, you will score well, give or take those odd little quirks of fate which echo the occasional cruelty of life itself. If you are playing badly, blame yourself if you can, not the greenkeeper.

The player on the first tee expects to be rewarded for good shots and will therefore take a certain amount of punishment for bad ones in his stride. But if his good shot gets bad results, his mood will change. He can master the irritation caused by odd little quirks because that is expected of a sportsmanlike character, but there is a limit to the bad luck which Fate hands out over a period. If the course supplements that basic ration with problems of its own, there will soon be some very unhappy golfers. Can we formulate guidelines for the man who is responsible for presenting 100 acres or more in a state which combines equity, beauty, challenge, interest and the ability to remain consistently that, rather than fluctuate with each application of fertilizer?

That is the first problem – fertilizer. How much? How often? What? When? A steady routine must be sought so that both grass and players know where they are. Players like greenness. Poa Annua likes it less. But Fescues do not look all that verdant at some seasons. And are they *really* hard-wearing even if they do give the sort of turf that classic shots require? The fertilizing programme adopted (which strongly affects the composition of turf) must feel its way through

Fig. 6.2   One of Ransomes' latest models, the Hydraulic 5/7, bestrides a low round on a flat seaside links on the east coast of England, cutting right up to the edge of the bunker. (Courtesy of Ransomes Sims Jefferies plc.)

conflicting opinions to the satisfaction of the majority. They will not be satisfied if they see the course green and vigorous for a special occasion and tired and yellow a month later: still less so if a starvation programme precipitates crisis conditions and they are told that it will all come right in two years' time.

Mechanical operations must also be on a regular footing so far as weather permits. Hollow tine cores or top-dressing should be notified in the clubhouse ahead of their appearance on the course.

Before operations involving much surface disturbance, the diary of visiting societies or local events likely to bring many visitors, should also be consulted.

Mowing should be regular enough to avoid significant difference in rough, fairway or elsewhere as between holes and days. Equal speed on greens must be provided through a consistent mowing schedule. Equality of green speed is, however, compounded by compaction, grass species, thatch and water. Soft greens of any type will not give true putting conditions at different times of the day; pitch marks, footmarks round the hole, and variation of speed complicate fair putting besides negating skill in applying spin to the ball. They present less challenge and may even reward a bad shot.

Players disapprove of unfair rewards even when they occur as an ordinary rub of the green; they dislike them still more if they occur through man-made conditions. Timing of watering in relation to local playing times and turf condition is therefore a vital decision.

While respecting all these factors, the greenkeeper has much more to do. There must be clear directions round the layout, with proper paths, tidy tees, and frequent changes of hole and tee positions for interest as well as to avoid wear.

Bunkers have to be neat enough for the golfer to know if he is in the hazard or not. But trimming edges should not constantly enlarge the sand area. The sand itself will be selected for good colour, clean non-binding texture, and absence of stone or foreign matter as well as for its price. Out of bounds and lateral water hazards will also be defined clearly.

On some courses autumn leaves must be cleared, on others, pine needles. All must go before they impinge on the player's equanimity.

Can the greenkeeper really achieve all this to keep his members happy? It seems very likely. They

(a)

(b)

(c)

Fig. 6.3   No. 18 at the Pals Golf Club on the Spanish Costa Brava.
(a) From the start of the fairway. (b) A pulled tee shot brings these trees into
calculation of the second shot. (c) Two bunkers guard the large green,
over 1000 m².

start every round with high hopes and will blame themselves to some degree before they blame the course. Once they start doing that, there is no going back. Conditions must be fair, smooth, moderately firm, attractive, tidy, understandable, challenging, rewarding and consistent throughout the 18 holes and the season.

Similar considerations apply when preparing a golf course specially for a tournament. Any temptation to push the design beyond what it can reasonably provide should be resisted. Trickery will immediately cause antipathy. Hole positions, tee positions, bunker positions, fairway widths must still be within certain norms. Similarly the condition of the course is not something to be left till the last few months; its preparation must start one or two years back with a steady programme of thoughtful maintenance following expert construction, though perhaps truly thoughtful maintenance will not need much modification.

Hole positions can go to the limit of the green design but the 5 yard rule should not be breached. Back tees not normally used should be firm and any invasive undergrowth or tree branches cut well back. Fairways can be waisted towards the end of the professional drive as low as 25 yards on level stretches but not less than 35 where there is a significant cross fall. However, this waisting should be related to the hole's strategy. The fairway centre should not be shifted to the right, for example, if the only place from which the green can be attacked is then in the rough.

The rough will no doubt be the subject of comment, generally unfavourable, because everyday practical considerations have largely effaced it on inland courses. But if there is no penal rough the player who fails to play the hole as designed but as he thinks may produce a birdie, should take half a shot or one shot more than the player who has played accurately.

By half a shot is meant that if on two occasions during successive rounds he drives into the rough at the same hole, he will get a par once and one over par once. There should be a situation, therefore, in which we can expect him to recover by extremely good play on one occasion but not twice running. Ideally the risk for those flirting with severe danger to achieve a birdie should be that much greater to give the greatest savour to the choice on the tee. But that is something which the hole either does or does not provide. Those responsible for preparing the course will already have had enough of analysis in deciding where the rough should be, and how long it should be, in relation to the optimum play of the hole over its length and its green design.

Even at the green, the price of failing to find it should be exacted, though relative to the length of the approach shot.

Putting surfaces will be tender enough to receive the properly struck approach from the correct spot on the fairway but firm enough to disappoint anything else. This condition is allied to the fast smooth surface which will emphasize the need for a well struck, well judged putt.

The best laid plans will go awry in tournaments with big galleries which trample the rough making it preferable to miss the fairway by 50 yards rather than five. Where this is likely to happen the Green Committee can only trust to the design of the hole to extract the penalty. And after all, some of the best remembered shots on television (and before it) have been those where the ball reappeared from perdition, carried damnation and plopped innocently on to the green as if nothing had happened. Let the Green Committee set a reasoned scene therefore; the drama will take care of itself.

6.6   A SINGLE GREEN

Where it is decided to do work by direct labour, the construction of a new green is normally the biggest task likely to arise during a Green Convener's term of office. It demands careful planning and preparation.

The plan should be prepared in the previous winter or spring. A level grid is required over the site so that existing and new contours can be related. There is generally a surveyor member who will undertake the preparation of the grid. It is probably wise to engage a golf course architect to prepare the plan, showing the projected contours. In other cases, Appendix 4 may be of assistance. But it is always wise to consult an agronomist as well.

A specification is also desirable, indeed indispensable, if an outside contractor is employed. However, if the work is to be done in the period September–December, the club's staff can generally manage the preparation and turfing or sowing, if hired machinery is brought in for turf cutting, earth-moving and cultivation.

(a)

(b)

Fig. 6.4 Stages in preparing the green. (a) Draining the foundation. (b) Starting to spread the stone. (c) Apron barrier to prevent incursion of undesirable rhizomes from outside. (d) Using the bunker-raking machine to smooth off the final surface mix. (Courtesy of Nigel Butler, The Country Club, Johannesburg.)

(c)

(d)

Next, consider access to the site and agree a route with the head greenkeeper. It will sometimes be preferable to accept a certain degree of damage, e.g. a single lorry track across a fairway, for the sake of getting all materials close to the job. But the route must be strictly controlled all the time it is in use because subsequent drivers may wander from the line given to the first. Tipping sand, peat and stone at a distance to save ruts will involve time-consuming reloading and repeated journeys with tractor and trailer. And because this will be done later in the year, it may lead to mud or more damage than a few lorries would have caused in dry weather. The earth mover will probably be a fairly small-tracked tractor with digging and loading gear, which will not cause much damage when it crosses fairways provided it keeps straight.

Everything should be done in this way to save time. You are operating with a fairly small ground staff. The weather in Autumn is uncertain (though it is the only time the work can be done in this way before the soil gets saturated) and it is important to get all the turf back by Christmas. There is nothing more depressing to ground staff and members than opening too much ground and seeing the job run on into Spring next year, especially as there are still routine tasks to be done on the rest of the course which cannot be neglected.

A temporary green will also have been prepared during the summer so that it could be in a reasonable condition by now and permit switching the turf from the old green to the new one, when the time comes, without much disturbance to play.

All the grass over the site of the new green will also have been cut so that turf can be readily stripped and reused using a turf-lifting machine (because that, too, will save hours of hand work). Arrangements will have also been made to alter the water system. The head greenkeeper has had time to organize his programme to fit in this extra task.

When turf is stripped from the site, make sure a big enough area is cleared. It is surprising how big an area is needed, especially for a built-up green, if the banks are to be graded out properly. As a rough guide, twice to three times the area of the putting surface will be needed; keep machines inside this limit.

It will be a month or two before the turf is relaid, so lay it out rather than roll or stack it. Otherwise there will be considerable discolouration.

Now remove the topsoil and place this to one side or at the back of the green, not on the approach which should be disturbed as little as possible.

Next form the new contours in the subsoil. If your filling material is imported, make sure that it is stable, and properly consolidated. Even if only levelling by cut and fill, see that the filling is done in layers each one firmed up before the next one goes on.

The bunkers and featuring should be done at the same time as the general formation. If they are added afterwards they seldom blend so well. Avoid anything that could, even remotely, be described as a 'pimple'. Smoothly flowing undulations on a broad scale will look much better. By all means introduce gentle folds into the putting area, but remember, as we noted earlier, that the more rolling the green surface the bigger the total area to provide adequate space for cutting the hole and distributing wear. The folds must not be so pronounced as to cause maintenance problems and they should not cause water to collect in hollows. Any major undulations should be followed right through each succeeding layer to give even depths.

Unless the subsoil is free-draining, next install the drains and the drainage layer – stone rejects blinded with ash or chippings or coarse sand. Even if the other greens on the course have no drainage layer, the amount of play today makes rapid drainage essential if your new green is to remain healthy. So you must look to the future. On a sandy or a light loam only amelioration may be necessary. Then subsoil cultivate the putting area as well as the surrounds of the new formation (and wherever the Drott has been) to relieve compaction. A rotovator will only make the situation worse if no subsoiling is done before it operates.

Now the topsoil can be spread. Whether from the old green or imported, ensure that it has the right degree of permeability by adding the appropriate amounts of sharp sand and peat. Your agronomist will advise on what these should be. Extend the soil-mix on to the approach, the surrounds and on to a site for a frost green if you can afford it. Modern consultants include more and more sand in their recommendations for greens and you may find your advise suggesting only sand and peat. But here again, do not try to calculate a mix without advice. There are so many variables that only the expert should handle them.

By now a month or more will have passed, leaving the rest of November to firm up the soil, prepare it, lay the turf, and give the final top-dressing. If the weather has caused delays (and never try to beat the weather by working when the soil is wet), December is still in reserve. The new green could be ready for play next May. It will still be rather uneven, but frequent top dressing will soon smooth it out if the turf has been well laid, including boxing if necessary. Most of the careful preparation, however, will be set at naught if the turf is matted, the soil is heavy or the quality is poor. If there is no hurry, sterilizing and sowing a good mixture of seed will be cheaper and eventually better. The new turf grown on nylon mesh over a special medium may otherwise be used, provided it contains only the grass strains actually sown.

A final word. Failing all the preparations, the plans, warning the members, organizing the ground staff and its programme, booking hired machinery, ordering materials and all technical advice – wait until next Autumn.

Appendix 1

Survey of the carry (pitch) of drives
carried out on behalf of the British
Association of Golf Course Architects
(B.A.G.C.A)

The survey was carried out on Saturday 19 April and Sunday 20 April 1975 between 09.30 and 18.00 during the Spring Meeting of Moor Park Golf Club on the 16th hole of their West Course by Raymond W. Read and George C. Moss. There was a following breeze of approximately 15–20 m.p.h. The run after pitching was an average of 15 yd.

Distances (yd)	No. of drives	%	No. of drives	%	Average %
Under 150	40	34.5	30	26.0	30.25
150–160	16	13.8	16	13.9	13.85
160–170	10	8.6	12	10.4	9.50
170–180	16	13.8	18	15.7	14.75
180–190	13	11.2	10	8.7	9.95
190–200	5	4.3	12	10.5	7.40
200–210	8	6.9	11	9.6	8.25
210–220	4	3.5	3	2.6	3.05
220–230	2	1.7	2	1.7	1.70
Over 230	2	1.7	1	0.9	1.30
	116	100.0	115	100.00	100.00

21 April 1975

Appendix 2

Length

A rough guide for estimating potential length after providing normal amenities is as follows:

	Area		Length	
	Acres	Hectares (rounded up)	Yards	Metres
A	90	37	5600–5800	5120–5300
B	100	41	5800–6000	5300–5490
C	110	45	6000–6200	5490–5670
D	120	49	6200–6400	5670–5850
E	130	53	6400–6600	5850–6040
F	140+	57+	6600–6800	6040–6220
G	150+	61+	6800+	6220+

These lengths will be exceeded on easy sites but will be reduced by physical obstacles or awkward boundaries which limit land use. The clubhouse area will need 3–4 acres ($1\frac{1}{4}$–$1\frac{3}{4}$ hectares) and a practice ground at least the same. These areas are minimal.

Extensions of the 9 hole courses will often be longer than this table suggests in the relative acreage because clubhouse parking, and sometimes practice ground, have already been provided.

Appendix 3

Green plans (Martin G. Hawtree)

Before tenders can be invited or quantities calculated, the green plan must be provided and measured. Sometimes a club-member with the appropriate training will undertake this if a golf course architect is not employed. In that case, the following article, prepared by Martin Hawtree for the British Association of Golf Course Architects, may be of assistance.

ON THE NEED FOR ACCURACY IN GREEN PLANS

One of the more severe tests of an architect's skill and workmanship is the control of a contractor who is both unknown to him and new to the field of golf course construction. Local politics may often require a small, near-by firm of contractors to be included on the Select List. More often than not such firms produce excellent work. Nevertheless, the architect must be confident at the start that his client will receive the benefit of the lowest tender, that his own ideas and requirements have been accurately conveyed through the Drawings and Contract Documents, and that the contractor has been given all the information he needs on which to base a fair and profitable price for the job. Indeed every new contract requires such an attention to detail, no matter how familiar the list of contractors can be expected to be.

Now this is a more important matter than simple clear conscience. If golf course architects are not merely to borrow the robes of their senior professions, then they have a duty to study accurate workmanship in both the interests of their clients and contractors. The mother profession of architecture arose in the mid-19th century amidst steady decline of building craftsmanship and sudden profusion of new architectural styles. If comparable circumstances have surrounded the birth of professional golf course architecture in this century, they are far from being self-evident either to the general or the golfing publics. Consider the matter of style. Today there are a good many *soidisant* golf architects, each with their own outlook and preferences. All pretend to be worshipping one god, Nature. But how manifold and vast is this. There are some who seek in their designs to imitate the whisperings of Aeolus or the wrath of Boreas; there are those who prefer glaciation as the model for their earthmovement; there are others who search for a fluvio-geomorphology; and there are still others who appear well satisfied with a major recording on the Richter scale.

Outside broad contrasts between American and European styles, or an occasional respect paid to the style of an old master, there is not as yet much conception or serious analysis of individual style in golf course architecture. It is certainly a measure of professionalism, the extent to which an architect can expect accurate pricing of his drawings as the lucid countenance of a personal style. This is not to say that there is no place for the last-minute wave of the arm on site, for lengthy site-meetings, and revised instructions. But hard, pre-contract work, imaginative forethought, and accurate draftsmanship are the necessary conditions for signifying style and building up a responsible profession.

How, then, can the architect be sure that the green plan expresses his ideas accurately and that he will be well satisfied with the finished result? Can he produce anything more than the green plan to assist the contractor?

The most primitive and clear form of stylistic, personal expression is the free-hand drawing. It is not often used today and sketching is perhaps an art worth cultivating if style is to be taken seriously. Some form of three-dimensional representation is nevertheless useful in the full appreciation of a green plan. A scaled axonometric would be a difficult drawing to produce, if not impossible; the only substitute being a form of subtle shading along the vanishing point of a low sun, similar to the shading of hill regions on older 1 inch Ordnance Survey Maps.

A more satisfactory method of perfecting a style and portraying architectural ideas is to produce a scale model. An old and much-tried material is green plasticine. Delightful, smooth-flowing contours can be achieved with this material. Modelling in plasticine is normally carried out at rather small scales and the interpretation of vertical heights can be a problem.

An easier material to work with, but less permanent, is moist sand. A fine—medium washed sand works well at the large scale of 1:100. At this scale it is relatively easy to introduce a vertical scale of 1:20 with four miniature ranging rods at the corners of the sand tray. A small palette knife is useful to smooth off contours and a standard paint-fixative sprayed on will help keep the model stable after the moisture has evaporated. The nature of the material does not encourage the very small-scale, sometimes rather fussy detail of a plasticine model, and in general conforms rather well to the true potentials and limitations of constructing a green with heavy machinery. Such a model is clearly not portable, and to be of any subsequent use to the architect or contractor it must be photographed. If the putting area is well firmed down, a silvery sand placed in the bunkers, and a strong side-lighting introduced, a good effect can be obtained with a tele-photo lens, fitted with a macro-converter.

The third technique is one used in large-scale landscape and geographic relief modelling. A material of uniform thickness is taken to represent a contour interval and can be cut into shapes with knife or fret-saw. In this way a properly contoured green-plan negative can be traced out on ply-wood or other material and each contour plateau cut out. It is not a technique for experimenting with forms or working up the details of a plan; it simply converts the contours to three dimensions. It is time-consuming so to model a large and complex green, but since the technique guarantees the accuracy of the vertical scale, it can be useful for simply and quickly modelling the existing site contours; one of the other modelling materials can then be used to form the green. If the bulk density of the wood and, for example, sand when dry, is known, then it is possible to check very roughly the quantities of cut and fill by weighing the quantity of ply wood 'cut', displacing an equivalent volume of water with the sand 'fill', converting back the scaled volumes after allowing for the difference between the horizontal and vertical scale.

Useful though these techniques may be for refining green designs, assisting inexperienced contractors and Clerks of Works, or discussing the client's requirements, they are time-consuming and expensive. In a round of 18 greens, one or two models may have to suffice, to indicate a general style. The ultimate instructional document is, therefore, bound to be the green plan itself. The plan will be of little use to a contractor unless it relates existing contours to proposed changes in level; the contractor will otherwise have to guess the quantities of cut and fill, which is neither fair on the contractor nor conducive to sound, competitive pricing. For this purpose a 60 × 40 m grid of levels at 10-m intervals will normally be adequate, set out along the axis of the centre line to the green.

Surveying greens in relation to a common bench mark or Ordnance Datum is laborious but indispensable for the resolution of any later contractual disagreements. Working from an accurate survey, the architect can then set to work with sketches, plasticine or sand, and begin to formulate the contour revisions in accordance with his conception of the hole. Drawings at a scale of 1:100 are useful to include all contouring details on surrounds and putting surfaces, drain-lines, and irrigation mains; but at this scale they are bulky and take time to draft. Certainly nothing smaller than 1:200 seems appropriate. From the plan, longitudinal- and cross-sections can be prepared to illustrate the build-up, drain-gradients, and relations of subsoil, stone layer (if present), and topsoil levels; although with a good plan, these are seldom necessary.

An accurate contour drawing, then, facilitates sound contractual work by the use of profiles; allows cut-and-fill quantities to be taken off simply; reduces considerable discussion on site and claims for extras; and if well drawn and coloured, provides a permanent record of the architect's intentions. As designers, golf course architects will be judged by the finished quality of their greens, not their plans; but by all who work with them they will be regarded as professional in relation to standards of thoroughness, clarity, and reliability. In addition, far from detailed plans and models being a chore and waste of effort, they will certainly assist in the demonstration of golf architectural style together with the control of its contractual realization as the cornerstone of any proper professional foundation.

Martin Hawtree

Appendix 4

Specimen pages:
Specification and Bills of Quantity

A. SPECIFICATION PAGES

Materials

Sand
This should be lime-free and have the characteristics required in the upper ranges of Zone 2 or the lower range of Zone 1 referred to in British Standard Specification 882 (Fine Aggregate). The sand should be sharp, washed, free from all stones and dirt.

Sand particle size should be between 0.25 mm and 1.00 mm for both bunker and topsoil mixes, with 75% of particles lying in the medium range of 0.25 mm to 0.60 mm.

Signed vouchers for all deliveries of sand should be available for inspection, as well as periodic weigh-bridge tickets to establish the bulk density of the sand, so that importing of sand for topsoil mixes prepared on a volumetric basis can be accurately monitored.

Peat
All peat used as a soil ameliorant or as a mulch, should conform to BS. 4156:1967. It shall be obtained from an approved source, be dark brown in colour, free from dirt and rubbish, neither slimy, nor too fibrous. Peat having a bulk density higher than 0.6 tonne/m^3 will not be accepted. If peat is purchased in a dried compressed state, it should be thoroughly broken up and wetted before mixing with sand and/or topsoil.

Topsoil
Imported topsoil shall be from an approved source, obtained from the top 150 mm of ground, clean, and free of all stones and other debris. It shall be fertile with a humus content.

Note No sand/peat/topsoil shall be brought on to site until samples and mixes have been examined and tested for hydraulic conductivity. Any topsoil brought on to site prior to these tests will be at the Contractor's own risk.

If supplies of the material run out before completion of work, any further requirement for sand/peat/topsoil should not be met before the same procedure for examination and testing has been carried out on the new source of supply.

Where top dressing is required use only those materials and in the same proportions as were used for the construction of greens. Where these materials are no longer available obtain the advice, sending samples if necessary, of the Sports Turf Research Institute as to a suitable top dressing.

Site soil
Where site soil is to be reused, it shall not be allowed to remain stacked for longer than 6 months. Carry out spraying if necessary to check weed germination and growth.

Aggregate
All materials for use as porous layers and drainage back fills should be clean, angular, of uniform particle size, and within the dimensions specified. Where a blinding layer of finer aggregate is required, the particle size (within the dimensions specified) should not be less than 1/7th of the diameter of the particle size of the larger aggregate below it. All blinding material shall be free of fines.

Drain pipes
Tile drains shall be Clayware (to B.S. 1196) or porous concrete (to B.S. 1194). Outlet pipes shall be of salt-glazed ware and shall comply with B.S. 65. The use of pipes which have been allowed to stand over winter, will not be permitted.

Chemicals

Chemical fertilizers and sprays are to be used only where specified. They shall conform in all respects to the mixture required and be applied strictly in accordance with the manufacturer's instructions. All distribution and spray equipment should be correctly calibrated beforehand, in the presence of the Clerk of Works or representative of the Golf Course Architect, if required. Application of fertilizer and sprays shall be supervised by the foreman and all damage caused by excess or drift will be made good at the contractor's own expense.

Earth movement

Topsoil removal

Scrape off all true topsoil from areas where greens, approaches, green surrounds, tees, and bunkers are to be basically formed in subsoil, and from those areas in the rough to be excavated for subsoil fill.

Scrape off all true topsoil from areas indicated where it is necessary to marry through the levels of adjoining fields along the line of original hedges or fences or walls. The topsoil shall be stripped to a width of 5 m either side of the original dividing line.

Stock-pile topsoil to avoid interference with subsequent operations – in the case of greens and tees to one side of or behind the green or tee area.

Ensure that no subsoil is mixed with the topsoil.

Subsoil grading

General

Following removal of topsoil and stock-piling to avoid interference with subsequent operations, adjust subsoil levels to the formations required by the Golf Course Architect. Subsoil grading will normally be done by 'cut and fill' filling in consecutive layers not exceeding 225 mm depth. Where impractical to adopt 'cut and fill' or where a subsoil deficit arises, subsoil surplus from other parts of the works shall be used and/or subsoil excavated from approved areas in the rough. All subsoil formations should be adequately firmed in layers by repeated tracking.

Greens, approaches, surrounds

The putting area will consist of an irregular shape averaging approximately 500 m², contoured to be free from moisture-collecting hollows. Where a drainage layer and sand/soil/peat mix is to be installed, the formation level of the putting area will be 300 mm below that of the subsoil level of the green surrounds, so that a subsoil retaining wall is formed to hold in place the porous layer and 125 mm of the topsoil mix. Where two tiers are required the intervening step will have a fall no steeper than 1 in 8.

Green surrounds will include informal banks in a variety of shapes, mounds, and hollows, with gradients no steeper than 1 in 4. This featuring, following the return of topsoil, shall marry imperceptibly into the putting surface and existing surrounding contours. No featuring shall be formed in such a manner that surface water tends to collect against or to one side of the mound or bank. Into some of these surrounding mounds, bunkers will be formed as described below. The Contractor should take care to maintain approved subsoil grades and featuring throughout subsequent operations.

Approaches will consist of an area approximately 250 m² in front of the green, contoured to marry in the new level of the putting surface with the existing levels in front of the green, following the return of topsoil. Where planned levels for the putting surface make it unnecessary for regrading the approach in subsoil, the approach should be disturbed as little as possible and should not be driven over by heavy machinery.

Tees

The outline of the tee may, according to the requirements and plans of the Golf Course Architect, either be rectangular or adapted to neighbouring contours to provide an informal shape generally aligned towards the axis of the hole but without straight edges precisely parallel to that axis. The front edge of the terrace will be 300 mm above the level of existing ground in front of the tee. Tees on descending ground will be terraced in two or three levels connected by intervening slopes of 1 in 5. All banks will be left not steeper than 1 in 4.

Bunkers

Bunkers will vary in area, plan, and elevation. The sand areas will average 75 m², shaped with an alternative concave and convex outline matched alternately by rising and descending external banking sloped off imperceptibly into external contours with a grade not steeper than 1 in 4. The sand face will vary between 30° and 40° from the horizontal. Floors will be gently sloped to evacuate any surface collection of water, or where drains are planned to the point of the drain outlet, after general approval of the shape by the Golf Course Architect. Bunkers in rising ground will be formed by excavation and removal of surplus. Bunkers on level or descending ground will be formed by depositing suitable material to form a mound. Allow 75 m³ average fill for formation of this mound. Allow for introducing minor contouring to deflect surface water away from the mouth of bunkers, particularly on down hill slopes.

Preparation of grassed areas

Subsoil cultivation

Subsoil cultivation using a tractor-drawn trailer type mole plough fitted with a subsoil shoe, e.g. Ransomes C1. The supporting bar for the subsoil shoe shall be vertical with a sharpened leading edge.

Implements fitted to the hydraulic linkage system of a tractor will not be approved unless demonstrated on site as capable of the specific work. Subsoil cultivate in the direction of maximum fall at no more than 600 mm centres and at a minimum depth of 450 mm. Take care not to work subsoil into topsoil.

Subsoil cultivation may be required on putting areas where there is no drainage layer, on green surrounds, tees, approaches, and all areas which have been stripped of topsoil, the cultivation to be executed twice, once *before* the return of topsoil, once *after* the return of topsoil. Single subsoil cultivation may be required on Fairway areas and Marginal Rough.

Take care not to subsoil cultivate in the vicinity of irrigation pipes and cable lines.

General preparation and sowing:
greens, tees, approaches and surrounds

Ploughing
Plough the putting area and approaches using a tractor-mounted plough taking care not to turn up subsoil or stone.

Cultivation
Cultivate all areas to produce a reasonably fine tilth. Relieve all compaction through the full topsoil depth and keep the areas free from weeds until seed bed preparation commences. Use tractor-mounted tine cultivators and disc harrows or approved hand-operated machinery (excluding rotary cultivators). Allow for handwork where the use of machinery is impracticable. Allow for eight cultivations, each cultivation comprising two passes, the second transverse to the first.

Maintain the desired levels and contours of all areas. Ensure that any marrying in of green banks with putting areas does not translocate any depth of topsoil from the putting area to the banks. Always maintain the shape and contours of the green through successive layers of subsoil, stone, blinding and topsoil.

B. BILLS OF QUANTITY PAGES

Bill no. III

Earth movement

Topsoil strip
1. Strip topsoil over sites of greens and surrounds as shown on Drawings. and stockpile at side or back of greens
Specification clauses: (35.1.3.4)
Average depth of strip 250 mm   45 000 m²

2. Strip topsoil over sites of tees and tee banks (35.1.3.4) and stockpile to side or back of tees
Average depth of strip 250 mm   20 000 m²

3. Strip topsoil over sites of borrow pits and stockpile alongside for subsequent respreading
Average depth of strip 250 mm   4 ha

4. EO Item 3 for transporting stripped topsoil to Greens 7 and 12, distances between 50 m and 150 m   100 m³

5. Strip topsoil over narrow strips to marry levels of adjoining fields average 4 m width 250 mm depth   800 m

Subsoil excavation formation and grading

6. *Greens* (37.1.2.3/S) (43/S)
   Form greens, featuring, wing bunkers, and approaches in subsoil by
   cut and fill and by fill transported from borrow pits (topsoil strip t.e.) to
   the dimensions, shapes and levels shown on the Green Drawings

Green no. 1	Cut and fill	150 m³
	Nett fill	700 m³
Green no. 2	Cut and fill	150 m³
	Nett fill	450 m³
Green no. 3	Fill	900 m³
Green no. 4	Cut and fill	50 m³
	Nett fill	950 m³

Bill no. V

Drainage

Greens

1. Excavate trenches 175 mm wide and average 250 mm deep in subsoil
base of putting areas to the pattern shown on the Green Drawings (45)   2100 m

2. Provide and lay 75 mm tile drains on a 25 mm bed of 10 mm aggregate (46.1)   2100 m

3. Backfill trenches with aggregate to subsoil formation level (48)   2100 m

4. EO Item 2 for angle junctions 75 mm on 100 mm (47)   150 No.

5. EO Item 2 for 75 mm–100 mm tapers   10 No.

6. Provide 1500 m³ single-sized aggregate (e.g. 25 mm) and spread 150 mm
    depth as porous layer over putting areas (51.1)   9150 m²

7. Provide 500 m³ aggregate (6 mm) spread 50 mm depth over layer and
    roll lightly (51.2)   9150 m²

Fairways
8. Clean out ditches (57)   400 m

9. Clean out ditch provide and lay 150 mm 'seconds' quality earthenware
    pipes surround with aggregate and cover with minimum 150 mm topsoil
    and grade to even levels (58.59)   40 m

10. Ditto, ditto, but 225 mm ditto, ditto   10 m

11. Form suitable outlets and inlets to piped lengths of ditches in concrete
     with base, head and wing walls (54)   10 No.

12. Form culverts as described (61)   25 m

13. Form new ditches 3 m × 0.9 m depth × 0.3 m bottom channel (60/S)   800 m

14. Excavate for provide and lay 75 mm tile drains average depth to invert
     600 mm (44;46)   500 m

Bill no. VI

Preparation and sowing
  8. Supply grass seed specified for Fairways and Rough (82/S) (28)   2850 kg
      Allow for labour
      Allow % for overheads and profit

Provisional
  9. Supply ground carbonate of lime for spreading on greens, tees, fairways
      and rough (77/S) (27)   33 t
      Allow for labour
      Allow % for overheads and profit

Subsoil cultivation
10. Subsoil cultivate surrounds of greens, approaches* at 600 mm centres
     at 300 mm depth (62, 62/S/2)   4.00 ha

11. Ditto, ditto tees and tee surrounds* at 600 mm centres (62/S/1)   1.75 ha

12. Subsoil cultivate at the appropriate time borrow areas, tracks, and other
     working or cultivated areas at 600 mm centres and at 350 mm depth
     following initial ploughing and discing (62.S.3)   11.00 ha

Soil mix
13. Using materials supplied under Items 1 and 2 of this Bill and Items

* A strip 10 m wide round toe of banks.

1 and 4 of Bill no. III produce a screened soil mix as described (volume loose) and transport to greens (65, 65S/1–5)   3200 m³

14. Spread soil mix from sides or rear over porous layers to an even firmed depth of 250 mm
Note No heavy or tracked vehicles will be allowed for this operation to avoid damage to drains or disturbance of porous layer surfaces   9150 m²

Amelioration, cultivation, stone picking
15. Using sand supplied under Item 1 spread and evenly incorporate with the top 50 mm of topsoil on tees and approaches to produce 100 mm depth of evenly ameliorated topsoil, using sand at the rate of 8 tonnes per 100 m² (66,66/S)   11 750 m²

16. Cultivate green approaches and tee surfaces to produce fine tilth (64/67)   11 750 m²

17. Cultivate green and tee banks to produce fine tilth (64,67)   45 600 m²

18. Pick off all stones of specified dimensions and remove from site (69)   57 350 m²

Provisional
19. Incorporate ground limestone supplied in Item 9 during cultivation at the rate of 20 kg/100 m² to greens and tees   16 400 m²

20. Ditto, ditto to approaches, green and tee banks   45 600 m²

21. Spread fertilizer supplied in Item 4 over putting areas at the rate of
    8.5 kg/100 m² (68)   9150 m²

22. Spread fertilizer supplied in Item 5 to green surrounds, tee banks,
    approaches and other areas at the rate of 375 kg/ha (68/S/1)   45 600 m²

23. Ditto, ditto to teeing areas at the rate of 70 g/m² (68/S/2)   7250 m²

24. Sow greens and approaches with proportion of grass seed mixture
    supplied in Item 6 (70/1/S/1)   40 000 m²

Appendix 5

Tree lists

A. Height and spread guide (in descending order of height)

Feet				Metres	
Height	Spread			Height	Spread
165	30	Sitka spruce	*Picea sitchensis*	50	10
130	120	Common beech	*Fagus sylvatica*	40	36
130	90	Horse chestnut	*Aesculus hippocastanum*	40	28
130	90	Common ash	*Fraxinus excelsior*	40	28
130	65	European larch	*Larix decidua*	40	20
130	65	Black Italian poplar	*Populus serotina*	40	20
130	65	Common lime	*Tilia europaea*	40	20
120	65	Sweet chestnut	*Castanea sativa*	37	20
115	110	Pedunculate oak	*Quercus robur*	35	36
115	50	Corsican pine	*Pinus nigra maritima*	35	15
100	80	London plane	*Platanus x hispanica*	35	25
100	50	Scots pine	*Pinus sylvestris*	30	15
100	65	Elm (English)	*Ulmus procera*	30	20
90	90	Holm oak (Evergreen)	*Quercus ilex*	27	27
90	70	Hornbeam	*Carpinus betulus*	27	22
90	60	Wild cherry (gean)	*Prunus avium*	27	18
80	65	Norway maple	*Acer platanoides*	25	20
80	65	White birch	*Betula pubescens*	25	17
80	50	Locust, false acacia	*Robinia pseudoacacia*	25	16
80	50	White willow	*Salix alba*	25	16
80	40	Field maple	*Acer campestre*	25	13

Tree lists

A. cont.

Feet				Metres	
Height	Spread			Height	Spread
80	60	Common walnut	*Juglans regia*	25	18
70	30	Common alder	*Alnus glutinosa*	22	10
75	70	Weeping willow	*Salix alba tristis* (*babylonica*)	23	21
70	40	White poplar	*Populus alba*	22	13
65	40	Mountain ash/rowan	*Sorbus aucuparia*	20	13
65	20	Holly	*Ilex aquifolium*	20	7
45	25	Hawthorn (quickthorn)	*Crataegus monogyna*	14	8
40	30	Whitebeam	*Sorbus aria*	12	9

This list is only a guide to help planning and spacing. The figures given are full ones. Not all trees reach their full potential because not all the factors: soil, exposure, moisture, competition, situation are favourable at the same time. As a general rule, related varieties developed for leaf or colour will be smaller. The catalogue should be consulted because nomenclature can vary. Spacing will also depend on the size planted and whether later thinning out is part of the scheme.

B. Notes on species and varieties (condensed from several authorities)

(× = Preferred)

	Acacia, false	(see Locust)
	Acer	(see Maple)
×	Alder (*Alnus*)	

	Common (*A.glutinosa*)	Very hardy prefers wet soils to dry; stands flooding.
	var. (*aurea*)	Yellow leaves till August; 30 to 40 ft (average).
	var. (*imperialis*)	Graceful tree with fine cut leaves; 30 to 40 ft (average).
×	Grey (*A.incana*)	Also useful for wet places; to 70 ft; very hardy.
	var. (*aurea*)	Yellowish young shoots and foliage, small.
	var. (*acutiloba*)	Deeply dissected leaves.
	var. (*pendula*)	Pendulous branches.
	Apple, wild	(see Crab)
	Ash (*Fraxinus*)	
	Common (*F. excelsior*)	Prefers good soil and chalk but tolerant; considerable debris; gross feeder but casts less shade than oak, beech.
	Manna (*F. ornus*)(*F. oxycarpa*)	Creamy white flowers; sometimes planted.
	var. Raywood	Smaller and attractive; 50 ft.
	Ash, mountain	(see *Sorbus*)
	Aspen	(see Poplar)
×	Beech (*Fagus*)	
	Common (*F.sylvatica*)	Well drained chalk and limestone soils; best in milder areas; good nurse but eventually dominant.
×	Copper/Purple –	Very fine specimen or grouped with green.
	var. (*F.s.purpurea*)	Colour variable.
×	Birch (*Betula*)	
	Silver (*B.pendula*)	Elegant; prefer light soils in drier parts but cover most golf course requirements.
×	White (*B.pubescens*)	Smaller than Silver Birch; to 60 ft, but sometimes a 'bush'; tolerates colder, wetter conditions.
×	Paper bark (*B.papyrifera*)	For a change.
×	River or black (*B.nigra*)	For river banks; ornamental in parks.
	Cherry (*Prunus*)	
	Wild cherry/gean (*P.avium*)	Fertile woodland soils especially over chalk but widely distributed; 65–80 ft (average). White flowers in April.
	Bird cherry (*P.padus*)	10–30ft. More common north of Midlands; flowers May for shorter period than above.

× Chestnut (*Aesculus*)
    Horse (*A.hippocastanum*)   Handsome white flowers; best in fertile soils; debris.
        (*A. × carnea* 'Briottii')
    Chestnut (*Castanea*)
    Sweet, Spanish –   Deep rich soil; mild climate; tends to untidiness in age; debris.
    (*C.sativa*)
× Crab (*Malus*)
    Apple (*M.pumila*)   20–30ft though often bushy; delicate fragrant flowers; May; many
                                     varieties; most showy in flower, fruit and/or leaf.

    Evergreen oak   (see Oak)
    Fir (*Abies*)
    Noble (*A.procera*)   Prefers deep well drained soils with moisture but stands fair acidity; less
                                     frost-tender than silver firs. Can grow to 150 ft.

    Goat willow   (see Willow)
× Hawthorn (*Crataegus*)
    Common –
    (*C.Monogyna*)   To 40 ft; stands exposure.
    (*C.oxyacanthoides*)   15–20 ft.
    var. (*C.o. Alba plena; C.o.*   Three handsome flowery types: double white = 'May', red and pink.
    Coccinea Plena; and C.o.   Other varieties have glossy leaves, good autumn colour etc.
    Rosea flore Plena)
× Hazel (*Corylus*)
    Common (*C.avellana*)   Humble, useful bush or small tree; 12–20 ft; purple variety perhaps less
                                     desirable; useful for divining rods.

    Holly (*Ilex*)   For occasional use (not variegated types) but rather gloomy; isolating
                                     hedgerow hollies will improve shape and view.

    Holm oak   (see Oak)
× Hornbeam (*Carpinus*)
    Common (*C.betulus*)   Moderate in demands on soil and moisture; survives frost hollows better
                                     than beech; does well in shade; varieties: *Columnare, Purpureus* explain
                                     themselves.

    Horse chestnut   (see Chestnut)

Laburnum
  Common (*L.anagyroides*)   Rarely found wild, occasionally semi-wild; poisonous to children, livestock;
  Scotch (*L.alpinum*)   varieties become more and more showy.
Larch (*Larix*)   Moist well-drained soil. Good spring colour. To 40 ft (average). Can grow
  European (*L.decidua*)   to 140 ft.
  Japanese (*L.leptolepis*)   Suitable upland courses. High rainfall. Thrives widely except dry climate,
    frost hollows, exposure; to 60 ft average.

  Hybrid (*L.x.eurolepis*)   Sometimes more successful on ground found extreme for the others. To
    about 60 ft.

× Lime (*Tilia*)   Large-leaved (*T. platyphyllos*) might be needed occasionally on park-type
  Common (*europaea*)   courses; common lime develops disagreeable burrs which sprout twigs
  Silver (*tomentosa*)   excessively. 30–100 ft.
Locust (*Robinia*)
  Black (*R.pseudoacacia*)   Fast growing when young but has wide ranging roots and suckers; tolerates
    poorer soils but in warmer climates.

× Maple (*Acer*)
  Field (*A.campestre*)   Common in South especially calcareous soils and in hedgerows; rarer in
    North; small leaves, golden in autumn; stands exposure; growth is moderate
    and slower in acid or wet soils.

  Norway (*A.platanoides*)   More common in South; tolerates pollution; ornamental in various soils;
    yellow gold in autumn; sometimes seen as escape from cultivation.

  Mountain Ash   (see *Sorbus*)
× Oak (*Quercus*)
  Pedunculate (*Q.robur*)   Good deep loams; not shallow, infertile or badly drained areas; more
    common in South.

  Sessile (*Q.petraea*)   More common west and north in shallower more sandy soils.
  Red (*Q.Borealis*)   Very handsome in season, especially on light soils. Fast growing.
  Turkey (*Q.cerris*)   Similar heights to native oaks but more pyramidal; less gnarled.
  Evergreen/Holm (*Q.ilex*)   Seaside tolerance but slow and can only be planted when small; also inland
    but not on cold wet soils.

  Osier   (see Willow)

Pine (*Pinus*)

×   Scots (*P.sylvestris*)   Thrives on dry, gravelly or sandy soils but widely adaptable; useful nurse. Avoid strong sea winds and wet moorland) 70 ft (average).

×   Corsican (*P.nigra*)   Lower elevations; sandy soil near sea; suits clay in south and east England.
      var. *calabrica*   Better on chalk than Scots; 80 ft (average).

×   Lodgepole (*P.contorta*)   Thrives on poor heaths, peats; best to withstand exposure; to 60 ft (average).

×   Austrian (*P.austriaca*)   Better on chalk; not suitable for damp soils, but again adaptable.

×   Mountain (*P.mugo*)   Stands great exposure; useful to mask ugly tee banks or to feature mounds.

    Plane (*Platanus*)   Leaf problem; not normally found wild in UK.

Poplar (*Populus*)

    White poplar   60–80 ft; road sides, river margins, especially in South; suckering habit; good screen.

    Grey poplar   Similar to *alba* but more erect and compact and more popular; silver grey
    (*P.canescens*)   flecked bark but also abundant and far reaching suckering.

×   Black poplar (*P.nigra*)   To 100 ft or more; rarely produces many suckers; often abundant on moist soils and river margins.

    Lombardy poplar   Slender, erect for avenues; tall screens.
    var. (*P.n.italica*)

    Aspen (*P.tremula*)   Trembling, rustling leaves go yellow/gold in autumn, but suckering a disagreeable feature; does not require rich soil.

×   Balsam   Streamsides, damp places but also clay; very fragrant in spring.
    (*P.trichocarpa*)
    (*P.gileadensis*)

    Prunus   (see Cherry)
    Quercus   (see Oak)
    Robinia   (see Locust)
    Rowan   (see *Sorbus*)
    Sallow   (see Willow)
    Service Tree   (see *Sorbus*)
    Sorbus

×   Mountain Ash/Rowan   20–30 ft. Grows in rocky glens and the lowlands, heaths, commons, most
    (*S.aucuparia*)   well drained soils; graceful habit, brilliant fruit; crimson leaves in autumn then orange/brown. Varieties: *Asplenifolia, Xanthocarpa*.

Whitebeam (*S.Aria*)	Up to 40 ft; variable species but prefers chalky or basic soils; abundant on chalk downs in Southern England; less common on other soils and in north. Varieties: *Decaisneana, Lutescens*.
Service tree	
True (*S.domestica*)	
Wild (*S.torminalis*)	Not common.
× Spindle (*Euonymus*)	
Spindle (*E.europaeus*)	Bush to 15 ft; common on chalk and limestone; good autumn colour; asiatic relatives are more showy especially *E.yedoensis*; the fruits are poisonous.
Spruce (*Picea*)	
Norway (*P.abies*)	Moist land, shallow peats, moderately fertile clays; Christmas tree.
Sitka (*P.sitchensis*)	Damp sites; stands exposure.
Sycamore (*Acer*)	
(*A.pseudoplatanus*)	Frost hardy; stands exposure including seaside; useful in shelter belts with pines; leaf problem close to play.
Walnut (*Juglans*)	
(*J.Regia*)	Likes light and warmth; severe frost harm; 65–80 ft.
Black walnut (*J.nigra*)	Faster; leaf debris is a problem of both types (squirrels generally get to the nuts first); Effingham G.C. Surrey, has many specimens in hedgerows.
Whitebeam	(see *Sorbus*)
× Willows (*Salix*)	
White (*S.alba*)	70–90 ft; river margins; deep moist soils.
var. (*S.a.vitellina*)	Orange/yellow twigs.
var. (*S.a.'Chermesina'*)	Orange/scarlet in winter.
var. (*S.a.coerulea*)	Rare in North and in Ireland; more spreading than typical *Salix alba*. Fast growing.
Crack (*S.fragilis*)	40–70 ft; olive-brown twigs; common in southern England.
White Welsh –	Orange/yellow twigs.
var. (*S.f.decipiens*)	Glossy ochre-coloured twigs.
Basford's	
var. (*S.f.basfordiana*)	Orange/yellow twigs.
var. (*S.f.sanguinea*)	Bright red twigs.

Purple osier (*S.purpurea*)	Shrub: 4–15 ft; slender yellowish or purple tinged twigs.
Violet (*S.daphnoides*)	Upright fast grower; broadens with age. Also *S.d. acutifolia*, which is semi-pendulus.
Goat willow (*S.Caprea*)	Bushy shrub; 10–30 ft; yellowish–green twigs = 'Palm'.
Common sallow (*S.cinerea*)	Bush or small tree to 40 ft; brown or reddish-brown twigs.
Osier (*S.viminalis*)	Small tree to 20 ft if left uncut; yellowish twigs.
Weeping (*S. vitellina, S. babylonica,* or *S. alba Tristis*)	Less vigorous; may have special applications where pendulous or semi-pendulous form is considered desirable.
Witch Hazel (*Hamamelis*)	
Japanese (*H.japonica*)	Shrub or small tree to 20 ft; flowers January–February; hardy but variable.
Chinese (*H.mollis*)	Flowers December–February.
	Both are ornamental but tolerable.

Appendix 6

Metric/Imperial conversions

Metric conversions, generally approximated, have been given in the text for quick comparisons. For greater accuracy and wider range, use the following table.

To convert	Multiply by
Acres to hectares	0.4047
Centigrade to Fahrenheit	$(°C \times 9/5) + 32$
Cubic metres to cubic yards	1.308
Cubic yards to cubic metres	0.765
Gallons Imperial to gallons (US)	1.200 95
Gallons US to Imperial	0.832 67
Hectares to acres	2.471
Kilograms to pounds	2.205
Litres to gallons Imperial	0.220
Litres to gallons (US)	0.2642
Litres to cubic yards	1.308×10^{-3}
Metres to yards	1.094
Pounds to kilograms	0.4536
Square metres to square yards	1.196

To convert	Multiply by
Square yards to square metres	0.8361
Yards to metres	0.9144

1 kilometre = 0.621 mile
1 mile = 1.609 kilometres

Bibliography

Books referred to or recommended for further reading

1887/8   John Bauchope (ed), *The Golfing Annual* Vols I–VIII. Horace Cox, 'The Field' Office, 346 Strand,
–1894/5 London WC.
1896   William Park, Jnr., *The Game of Golf*. Longmans Green & Co., London, New York and Bombay.
1898   Garden G. Smith, *The World of Golf*. A.D. Innes and Company Ltd, London.
1902   J.H. Taylor, *Taylor on Golf*. Hutchinson & Co., Paternoster Row, London.
1903   John L. Low, *Concerning Golf*. Hodder & Stoughton, 27 Paternoster Row, London.
1905   Harry Vardon, *The Complete Golfer*. Methuen & Co., 36 Essex St., London WC.
1906   Horace G. Hutchinson (ed), *Golf Greens & Greenkeeping*. Country Life Ltd, Tavistock St., London WC.
         and George Newnes Ltd., Southampton St., London London WC.
1908   James Braid, *Advanced Golf*. Methuen & Co., 36 Essex St., London WC.
1912   Martin H.F. Sutton (ed), *The Book of the Links*. W.H. Smith & Son, 55 Fetter Lane, London EC.
1912   Harry Vardon, *How to Play Golf*. Methuen & Co., 36 Essex St., London WC.
1920   Dr. A. Mackenzie, *Golf Architecture*. Simpkin, Marshall, Hamilton, Kent & Co. Ltd, 4 Stationers' Hall
         Court, London EC4.
1922   Major Guy Campbell, *Golf for Beginners*. C. Arthur Pearson Ltd, Henrietta St., London.
1926   Robert Hunter, *The Links*. Charles Scribner's Sons, New York and London.
1927   George C. Thomas Jr., *Golf Architecture in America*. The Times–Mirror Press, Los Angeles.
1928   E. Plumon, *Annuaire des Golfs du Continent*. Guides Plumon, 14 Rue Seguier, Paris 6.
1929   H.N. Wethered and T. Simpson, *The Architectural Side of Golf*. Longmans Green & Co., London,
         New York and Toronto.
N.D.   Colonel S.V. Hotchkin M.C., *Principles of Golf Architecture*. E.R.V. Knox, South Africa.
1933   Martin A.F. Sutton F.L.S., F.R.S.A., *Golf Courses, Design, Construction & Upkeep*. Sutton & Sons Ltd,
         Reading.
1952   Bernard Darwin *et al.*, *A History of Golf in Great Britain*. Cassell & Company Ltd, London.
1968   Joseph S.F. Murdoch, *The Library of Golf 1743–1966*. Gale Research Company, Detroit.
1973   Peter Dobereiner, *The Glorious World of Golf*. The Hamlyn Publishing Group Ltd, London, New York,
         Sydney and Toronto.

1975   Donald Steel and Peter Ryde (eds), *The Shell Encyclopaedia of Golf*. Ebury Press and Pelham Books Ltd, London.
1976   Pat Ward-Thomas and Iain Parsons (eds), *The World Atlas of Golf*. Mitchell Beazley Publishers Ltd, Shaftesbury Avenue, London W1V 7AD.
1977   George McPartlin and The Golf Development Council, *Golf Centres, a planning guide*. The Golf Development Council, 3 The Quadrant, Richmond, TW9 1BX.
1980   F.W. Hawtree, *Elements of Golf Course Layout & Design* (second edition). The Golf Development Council, 3 The Quadrant, Richmond, TW9 1BX.
1981   Geoffrey Cornish and Ronald E. Whitten, *The Golf Course*. The Rutledge Press (division of W.H. Smith Publishers Inc.), 112 Madison Avenue, New York, NY 10016

Greenkeeping

1962   Musser, H.B. *Turf Management* (revised edition) A.U.S.G.A. Publication, McGraw Hill Book Company Inc., New York and Toronto.
1970   Madison, John H., *Principles of Turfgrass Culture*. Van Nostrand Reinhold Company, New York.
1973   Beard James B., *Turfgrass: Science and Culture*. Prentice Hall, Inc., Englewood Cliffs, N.J.
1977   Dawson R.B., *Practical Lawncraft* (revised edition) Crosby, Lockwood Staple, London.
1978   Escritt J.R., *ABC of Turf Culture*, Kay & Ward Ltd, London.
1982   Cornish G.S. and Whitten, R.E., *The Golf Course*, The Rutledge Press, New York.

Greenkeeping periodicals

Annual
The Journal of the Sports Turf Research Institute. Bingley, Yorks.

Quarterly Bulletin
Sports Turf Bulletin. The Sports Turf Research Institute, Bingley, Yorks.

Monthly
Golf Greenkeeping and Course Maintenance. *Official Magazine of the British Golf Greenkeepers Association*, Wharfedale Publications Ltd., P.O. Box 12, Wetherby, West Yorkshire LS22 4SR
Greenkeeper. A. Quick & Co. Ltd, 121–123 High Street, Dovercourt, Harwich, Essex.

Parks, Golf Courses & Sportsgrounds. Clarke & Hunter (London) Ltd, 61 London Road, Staines, Middlesex, TW18 4BN.
Turf Management. Michael J. D. Alderson & Golf World Ltd, Millstream House, 41 Maltby Street, London, SE1 3PA.

————————

Green Section Record. The United States Golf Association, Golf House, Far Hills, NJ 07931.
Golf Course Management. The Golf Course Superintendents Association of America, 1617 St. Andrews Drive, Lawrence, Kansas. 66044.
The Greenmaster. Official Publication of the Canadian Golf Superintendents' Association, 698 Weston Road, Suite 32, Toronto, Ontario M6N 3R3.

Several informative publications from the National Golf Foundation, 707 Merchandise Mart, Chicago Ill. 60654, cover planning, construction, irrigation, promotion, tree planting, Par 3, Driving Ranges and the Club House.

Index

Abercromby, J.F., 34
Aberdeen (University), 14
Addington, 33, 34
Addington Court, *viii*, 132
Addison, 11
Allan Taylor, 35, 36
Alison, C.H., 27
Anderson, J.R., 138
Antwerp, Royal, 30
Auckland, N.Z., 123, 164
Augusta National, 138

Bassett, Southampton, 31
Baule, La, 164
Berkshire, The, 95
Bermuda Grass, 99
Bill of Quantities, 145, 147, 148, 151, 152, 189–194
Birkdale, Royal, *viii*, 118, 125
Blackheath, Royal, 6, 7, 8, 10
Blainroe, 53
Blind holes, 13, 25, 55
Braid, James, 23, 24, 30, 34
Brown, Horatio, 37, 141
Bruntsfield, *viii*
Bunkers
    banks, 23, 26
    behind greens, 26, 112
    built up, 112, 114, 118
    definition, 168
    economy of, 18, 56
    faces, 17, 37, 118, 120

location, 15, 20, 21, 22, 23, 24, 25, 26, 45, 111, 122
size, 118
specification, 187
style, 38, 112, 115, 118, 127, 133, 180
variety, 24
see also Hazards
Burnham and Berrow, 52, 138
Burnham Beeches, *vii*
Buttes Blanches, Les (Ghent), 126

Cabo Negro, Royal Morocco, 92
Campbell, Sir Guy, 34, 35
Carnoustie, 9
Castle Howard, 11
Chamberlain, Cyril, *viii*
Clerk of Works, 154, 155
Colt, H.S., 22, 24, 26, 72, 118, 138
Conditions of Contract, 147, 149
Copt Heath, 118
Construction, 145–155, 171–176, 179–182
Cornish, Geoffrey, 3, 206
Cotton, Henry, 36
Cultivation, 188
Cynodon, 99

Darwin, Bernard, 32
Dornoch, 3, 11
Downing, M.F., 11
Downshire G.C. Easthampstead, 142

Drainage, 149, 150, 152, 172, 175, 184, 190, 191
    surface, 104, 106, 144
Drawings, 153, 179–182
Dunn, Tom, 12, 50
Düsseldorf, 50

Earth movement, 185
Edgbaston, 118
Effingham, 201
El Prat, Barcelona, 72
Ellis, Jim, *viii*
Eltham, 10
Etiquette, 159–162

Fairways, 96, 122, 123, 124, 150, 170
Featuring, *see* Greens
Federación Española de Golf, 81
Fertilizing, 185
Formby, 164
Fowler, H., 22, 24, 119
Foxhills, 93, 129
Frilford Heath, *vii*
Furniture, 163, 164, 165

Gaisford St. Lawrence, Christopher, 61
Gibraltar, 11
Gleneagles, 5, 133
Golf Course Architects, British Association of, *vii*, 39

Golf .Courses
  Addington, 33
  Addington Court, *viii*, 132
  Antwerp, 30
  Auckland, 123, 164
  Augusta National, 138
  Baule, La, 164
  Berkshire, The, 95
  Birkdale, Royal, *viii*, 118, 125
  Blackheath, Royal, 6, 7, 8, 10
  Blainroe, 53
  Bruntsfield, *viii*
  Burnham and Berrow, 52, 138
  Burnham Beeches, *vii*
  Buttes Blanches, R.G.C. Les, (Ghent), 126
  Cabo Negro, Royal, 92
  Carnoustie, 9
  Copt Heath, 118
  Dornoch, 3, 11
  Downshire, 142
  Düsseldorf, 50
  Edgbaston, 118
  Effingham, 201
  El Prat, 72
  Eltham, 10
  Formby, 164
  Foxhills, 93, 129
  Frilford Heath, *vii*
  Gibraltar, 11
  Gleneagles, 5, 133
  Goodwood, 66, 135
  Harborne, 118
  Hardelot, 30
  Hill Barn (Worthing), 135, 136

  Hillside, *viii*
  Howth Castle, Dublin, 61
  Hoylake, 12, 20, 33, 94
  Humewood, 34
  Huntercombe, 98
  Ifield, *vii*
  Johannesburg, Country Club, 138, 172, 173
  Johannesburg, Royal, 138
  Killarney, 34, 90, 103
  La Baule, 164
  La Manga, 54, 121
  Leeds Castle, 35
  Leith, 6, 50, 165
  Lickey Hills, Birmingham, 31
  Liège, 30
  Limpsfield Chart, 10
  Le Prieuré, 105
  Le Touquet, 131
  Lindrick, *viii*, 113
  Liphook, 34
  Luffness, 9, 166
  Macauvlei, 34
  Machrihanish, 12
  Manga, La, 54, 121
  Marrakech, 138
  Merion, USA, 143, 144
  Mid-Surrey, Royal, 26
  Monte Carlo, 68
  Moor Park, 115, 116, 117, 177
  Morfortaine, 30
  Mortonhall, *viii*, 44, 140, 146
  Mount Mitchell Lands (N. Carolina), 164, 165
  Muirfield, 12, 34, 40, 118
  Murrayfield, 38

  Nairn, 85, 94
  North Devon, Royal, 33, 34, 166
  Pals, 130, 169
  Pau, 11
  Pebble Beach, 94, 95
  Pennant Hills, Sydney, 138
  Perth, 10
  Pine Valley, 40
  Portmarnock, 88, 93
  Prestatyn, 52
  Prestbury, 126, 138
  Prestwick, 34
  Prieuré, Le, *viii*, 105
  Royal Birkdale, *viii*, 118, 125
  Royal Blackheath, 6, 7, 8, 10
  Royal North Devon, *see* Westward Ho!
  Royal Salisbury (Zimbabwe), 82, 164
  Rye, 34
  St. Andrews, 6, 12, 20, 22, 33, 34, 43, 52, 94, 100, 108
  St. Cloud, 110
  St. George's, Royal, Sandwich, 34
  St Nom la Bretèche, *viii*, 55, 86
  Salisbury, Royal (Zimbabwe), 82, 164
  San Cugat, 72
  Saunton, 34
  Skegness, 34
  Southampton, Bassett, 31
  South Staffordshire (Tettenhall), 138
  Spa, 30
  Sunningdale, 34, 127
  Tandridge, 102
  Tours, 49
  Trevose, 34

Troon, Royal, 109
Turnberry, 33, 41
Valcros, 68
Walton Heath, 22, 33, 119
Waterloo, Royal, 60
Wentworth, 110
Western Gailes, 52
West Hill, 33
West Lancashire, 90, 164
West Sussex, 34, 43
Westward Ho!, 33, 34, 166
Wimbledon, 12
Woking, *vii*, 32
Woodcote Park, *vii*
Woodhall Spa, 34
Worplesdon, 33
Golf Course Measurements Ltd., 39,
      177
Golf Development Council, *vii*, 47,
      157, 206
Golf Greenkeepers Associations, *vii*,
      157, 158, 206, 207
Golf Illustrated, 14
Golfing Annual, The, 8–11
Goodwood, 66, 135
Graves R., 11
Greenkeeper Training Committee,
      157
Greenkeeping, 17, 27, 32, 35, 42, 57,
      58, 84, 85, 91, 95, 120, 132, 139,
      141, 148, 151, 156–159,
      166–176
Greens
   area, 13, 16, 24, 25, 32, 36, 57, 91, 93,
      94
   bunkering, 23, 122

entrance, 23, 25, 33, 94, 139
featuring/formation, 25, 26, 33, 35,
      61, 87, 89, 90, 101, 102, 104,
      106
gradient/levels, 13, 27, 32, 33, 55, 91,
      93, 97, 99, 100, 102
location, 13, 14, 22, 25, 55, 57, 61,
      87, 90, 91
orientation/outline, 32, 55, 95, 97,
      101, 122
par 3/pitch and putt, 63
plans, 91, 92, 178, 179, 180, 181, 182
reconstruction, 171–176
specification, 186
stock types, 107, 109, 110
temporary, 174
visibility, 13, 32, 89, 102
18th, 12, 59, 93
Gutty, ball, 25, 28

Harborne, 118
Hardelot, 30
Haskell, ball, 25, 28
Hawtree, F.G. and Taylor, J.H., 31,
      85, 118
Hawtree, Martin, 98, 178
Hazards (see also Bunkers)
   artificial, 16, 17, 18
   definition, 16, 17, 168
   location, 9, 13, 15, 18, 20, 22, 23, 25,
      26, 63
   penalty, 9, 13, 15
   trees, 13, 17, 35, 96, 130, 139
   types, 9, 10, 13, 15, 16, 17, 22, 24, 25
   visibility, 13, 15, 21, 55

Head Greenkeeper, 154, 156, 157,
      158, 159
Herrington, George, *viii*
Hill Barn (Worthing), 135, 136
Hillside, *viii*
Honourable Company of Edinburgh
      Golfers, 165
Horn, Douglas, *viii*
Hotchkin, Col. S.V. (M.C.), 34
Howth Castle, Dublin, 61
Hoylake, 12, 20, 33
Humewood, S.A., 34
Huntercombe, 98
Hutchison, Major C.K., 34

Ifield, *vii*

James II, 49
Jiggens, A.H.F., 147
Johannesburg Country Club, 138, 172,
      173
Johannesburg, Royal, 138
Jones, Robert Trent, 37

Killarney, 34, 90, 103
Knekkerbroek, Franz, *viii*

Lacey, Arthur, *vii*
Ladies Golf, 73, 81, 83
La Baule, 164
La Manga, 54, 121
Layout, 12, 14, 19, 22, 24, 25, 27, 30,
      37, 46–61, 87, 178
Leeds Castle, 34
Leith, 6, 49, 50, 165

Length of courses, 9, 19, 24, 34, 36, 40, 42, 47, 50, 51, 52, 54, 55, 58, 59, 61, 62, 63, 71, 81, 130, 178
Length of holes, 10, 12, 18, 19, 21, 24, 26, 27, 33, 34, 56, 59, 83, 93, 94, 102
Length of shots, 15, 19, 27, 39, 177
Le Prieuré, Paris, *viii*, 105
Lickey Hills, Birmingham, 31
Liège, 30
Limpsfield Chart, 10
Lindrick, *viii*, 113
Liphook, 34
Longhurst, Henry, 30, 32
Low, John L., 19, 24, 39, 122
Luffness, 9, 166

Macauvlei, 34
Macavoy, Ted, *viii*
Machin, Bill, *viii*
Mackenzie, Dr. Alistair, 26, 55, 108
Mackenzie Ross, 41
Machrihanish, 12
Marrakech, 138
McPartlin, George, *vii*
Merion, USA, 143, 144
Metric/Imperial Conversions 203, 204
Mid-Surrey, Royal, 26
Monte Carlo, 68
Moor Park, 115, 116, 117, 177
Morfontaine, 30
Morris, George 12
Morris, Old Tom, 11, 12
Morrison, J.S.F., 27
Mortonhall G.C., *viii*, 44, 140, 146

Mount Mitchell Lands (North Carolina), 164, 165
Muirfield, 12, 34, 40, 118
Murrayfield, 38

Nairn, 85, 94
Nesbit's Golf Year Book, 19
North Devon, Royal, *see* Westward Ho!

Pals, Costa Brava, 130, 169
Par 3, 62, 63, 97
Park, Willie, Jnr., 12, 14, 16, 28, 98
Pate, Douglas, *viii*
Pattisson, 35, 36
Pau, 11
Peat, 183
Pebble Beach, 94, 95
Pennant Hills, Sydney, 138
Penncross Bent, 99
Perth, 10
Pine Valley, 40
Pitch and Putt, 63
Portmarnock, 88, 93
Practice ground/green/bunkers, 35, 59
Prestatyn, 52
Prestbury, 126, 138
Prestwick, 34
Price, Uvedale, 37
Prickett, Charles, *vii*
Prieuré, Le, Paris, *viii*, 105
Professional Golfers Association, 2, 157
Public courses, 54, 58, 61, 73, 154
Pulborough (West Sussex), 34, 43

Ransomes (Ipswich), *viii*, 5, 156, 167

Read, Raymond, *viii*, 177
Repton, Humphrey, 37
Rodriguez, Chi Chi, 50
Ross, Donald, 3
Ross, Mackenzie, 41
Rough, 10, 25, 124, 125, 126, 150, 170
Royal Birkdale, *viii*, 118, 125
Royal Blackheath, 6, 7, 8, 10
Royal North Devon, *see* Westward Ho!
Royal St. George's Sandwich, 34
Royal Salisbury (Zimbabwe), 82, 164
Ruston-Bucyrus, 35
Rye, 34

Safety, 42, 43, 48, 62, 63, 162, 163
St. Andrews, 6, 12, 20, 22, 33, 34, 43, 52, 94, 100, 108
St. Cloud, 110
St. George's, Royal, Sandwich, 34
St. Nom La Bretèche, *viii*, 55, 86
Salisbury, Royal (Zimbabwe), 82, 164
San Cugat, Barcelona, 72
Sand, 111, 168, 183
Sarel, Major, 95
Saunton, 34
Scoop, Horse, 6, 29
Shelters, 164
Short holes, 16, 21, 62, 97
Simpson, Tom, 30, 31, 32, 99, 102
Sisis, 156
Skegness, 34
Smith, Garden G., 14
Smith, Harry, *viii*
South Staffordshire (Tettenhall), 138
Spa, 30
Spanish Golf Federation, 81

Specification, 145, 149–151, 171, 183–188
Sports Turf Research Institute, 157, 206
Stutt, J.R., 24
Subsoil Cultivation, 155, 187, 188, 192
Sunningdale, 34, 127

Tandridge, 102
Taylor, J.H., 18
Tees
　alternative, 39, 55, 56, 57
　area, 16, 25, 37, 72, 73
　back, 54, 66
　banks, 68, 69, 70, 75, 77, 78, 79, 80
　first tee, 12, 14, 24, 59, 85, 86, 87, 166
　ladies, 73, 81, 83
　levels, 12, 16, 63, 74, 75
　location, 16, 25, 27, 35, 57, 59, 61, 65–72
　mats, 62, 63, 83, 84
　orientation, 16, 77, 78

plan, 55, 56, 57, 71, 75, 76, 77, 78
slopes, on, 68, 69, 70, 71
specification, 186, 187
trees, in, 66, 67, 68, 132
visibility, 66, 72
Tenders, 147
Tournament preparation, 168, 170
Tours, 49
Trees/tree planting, 17, 56, 63, 96, 116, 123, 126–139, 151, 152, 195–202
Trevose, 34
Troon, Royal, 109
Turnberry, 33, 41

Uvedale Price, 37

Valcros, 68
Vanbrugh, Sir John, 11
Vardon, Harry, 25, 26
Visibility, 13, 21, 25, 32, 55, 67, 81, 89, 90, 97, 102, 113, 114, 143, 164

Walton Heath, 22, 33, 119
Water features, 48, 56, 94, 103, 128, 139–144
Water supply, 16, 48, 56, 57, 100, 152
Wentworth, 110
Western Gailes, 52
West Hill, 33
West Lancashire, 90, 164
West Sussex, 34, 43
Westward Ho!, 33, 34, 166
Wethered, H.N., 31, 32
Whitall, A.G., *vii*
Whitten, R.E., 3, 206
Wilson, George, *viii*, 105
Wimbledon, 12
Woking, *vii*, 32
Woodcote Park, *vii*
Woodhall Spa, 34
Worplesdon, 33

Yates, John, & Co. Ltd, 29